FURMAN v. GEORGIA

11/06/97

Furman v. Georgia

THE DEATH PENALTY AND THE CONSTITUTION

by
Judge Burt Henson
and
Ross R. Olney

Historic Supreme Court Cases
FRANKLIN WATTS
A Division of Grolier Publishing
New York London Hong Kong Sydney
Danbury, Connecticut

Photo credits ©: AP/Wide World Photos: pp. 28, 41, 99, 101; Collection of the Supreme Court of the United States: p. 66, 86 (Chase LTD); Corbis-Bettmann: p. 33; Impact Visuals: pp. 110 (David Rae Morris), 113, 115; Magnum Photos: p. 91 (Steve McCurry); Ossining Historical Society: pp. 38, 47; Richard Nixon Library: p. 63; Savannah Morning N   e   w   s   : p. 18; Supreme Court Historical Society: p. 76; UPI/Bettmann: p. 71.

Library of Congress Cataloging-in-Publication Data

Henson, Burt M. 1926–
    Furman v. Georgia: the death penalty and the constitution / by Burt Henson and Ross R. Olney.
        p. cm. — (Historic Supreme Court cases)
    Includes bibliographical references and index.
    Summary: Discusses the history of capital punishment, explains the United States Supreme Court's decision in Furman v. Georgia, and explores the impact of this case.
    ISBN 0-531-11285-3
    1. Georgia—Trials, litigation, etc.—Juvenile literature. 2. Furman, William Henry—Trials, litigation, etc.—Juvenile literature. 3. Capital punishment—United States—Juvenile literature. 4. Capital punishment—Georgia—juvenile literature. [1. Georgia, Trials, litigation, etc. 2. Furman, William Henry—Trials, litigation, etc. 3. Capital punishment.] I. Olney, Ross Robert, 1929– . II. Title. III. Series
KF228.F87H46 1996
345.758'0773—dc20   96-16022
[347.5805773]   CIP AC

FURMAN v. GEORGIA

CONTENTS

Chapter 1

A FATAL ENCOUNTER

William Henry Furman was frightened as he prepared to force his way through the back door of the house at 508 West 63rd Street. He even admitted that fact to himself. It was August 11, 1967, and times were tough in Savannah, Georgia. Furman needed the money that he would get when he sold the loot he planned to steal. He knew that he wouldn't be able to sell the stolen goods for anything near what they were worth, but he'd take whatever money he could get.

Sweating nervously as he worked on the door, Furman hoped things would go smoothly. It was dark and quiet in the middle-class neighborhood, and he was certain that he hadn't been seen. He wanted no trouble. The house was dark, and he was sure nobody was home.

Furman, an African American, was also aware of what happened to black men who were caught stealing from white men's homes in the South. Civil rights were only beginning to mean something in

1967. It was still true that if you were an African-American, you were probably wrong in the eyes of the authorities. Black lawbreakers, Furman knew, were routinely punished much more severely than whites for the same offenses.

He had no intention of getting caught or even confronting the home owner. That was the last thing Furman wanted. Get in, grab whatever valuables he could carry, and make a quick getaway without being noticed. That was the plan.

Furman knew what he was doing was a serious crime. But he also understood that it would be a rather minor offense in the big picture of crime. It was, after all, only a simple house burglary with nobody at home. A few possessions would be taken and that would be that. Nobody would be hurt, and some insurance company would probably cover the home owner's losses. No real harm would be done, he thought, and he would have some money in his pocket.

If what was about to occur had not happened, Furman's crime would long since have been forgotten by almost everybody. But what happened did happen. And the crime has not been forgotten—not by lawyers, judges, legal experts, or law students and certainly not by the victims and Furman himself.

William Furman was twenty-six years old and had completed only the sixth grade. He had no idea, as he nervously tried to break into the house, that he was about to make legal history. His minor crime was going to become a serious crime in the next few seconds, and, later, a very significant crime.

An inexperienced thief, Furman had no knowledge of the legal system. If he had, he probably would have abandoned the break-in and gone home. Furman's crime started out as a simple burglary but ended up worse than anything he could

glary but ended up worse than anything he could have possibly imagined. If things had worked out as he had planned, Furman would have broken in and stolen some property. He would probably have gotten away with it. If he had been caught, he would have paid for his crime with a few months in jail, and perhaps he would have decided never to try burglary again. But things don't always work out as planned.

Furman may have believed that nobody was in the dark house, but William Micke, his wife, and their five children were home asleep. Micke, a twenty-nine-year-old Coast Guard petty officer, heard the noises that Furman was making while trying to break in, and he got out of bed to investigate. What exactly happened in the next few moments is unclear. Furman later claimed that he panicked, fired a shot through the door, and then ran. Evidence at the trial suggested that Furman actually entered the house, was surprised by William Micke in the kitchen, and then ran for the door. The evidence also suggested that Micke slammed the door behind Furman, who shot through the door from outside before running away. Lanell Micke, the wife of the victim, called the Savannah police. They promptly responded and found William Micke lying dead on the kitchen floor. An officer spotted someone walking out of a wooded area near the Micke house. He followed the person, who suddenly began running. A call went out for backup, and more officers rushed to the scene. Rain was falling, which enabled the police to follow the person's muddy footprints. The trail of footprints led to a house. The police found William Henry Furman trying to hide under the house, which turned out to be his own home. The officers

Appearing before Judge Dunbar Harrison in the Chatham County Courthouse, Furman was indicted and formally charged with murder.

Furman could not afford to hire a lawyer, so Judge Harrison appointed attorney B. Clarence Mayfield of Savannah, Georgia, to represent him. The Supreme Court had ruled in *Powell v. Alabama* (1932) that poor defendants facing death sentences had a constitutional right to legal representation. The Court expanded this ruling in *Gideon v. Wainwright* (1963), holding that all poor defendants had a constitutional right to legal representation at their trial.[1] Because of these landmark decisions, Furman had an attorney to defend him against the murder charge.

Contemplating an insanity defense, Mayfield petitioned the court to order a psychiatric examination for his client, expressing concern "as to the extent of [Furman's] ability to realize the gravity of his actions." Mayfield hoped to make a plea of not guilty by reason of insanity. This defense required proof that Furman was so mentally ill that he did not understand the difference between right and wrong at the time he committed the crime.

On October 24, 1967, Judge Harrison granted Mayfield's petition and ordered Furman committed to the Georgia Central State Hospital for a psychiatric examination. He was to remain there until the examination was complete. On February 28, 1968, the superintendent of the state hospital at Milledgeville, Georgia, filed a report detailing the results of Furman's examination. The superintendent wrote:

> *This patient should retain his present diagnosis of Mental Deficiency, Mild to Moderate, with Psychotic Episodes associated with Convulsive Disorder. It was also agreed that*

with Psychotic Episodes associated with Convulsive Disorder. It was also agreed that at present the patient is not psychotic, but he is not capable of cooperating with his counsel in the preparation of his defense. We feel at this time that he is in need of further psychiatric hospitalization and treatment. He will be re-evaluated at a later date and presented to the staff again for a decision as to his final disposition.

On April 15, 1968, the superintendent reported the results of the hospital staff's reassessment of Furman's condition: "An evaluation has been made by our staff and a diagnosis of Mental Deficiency, Mild to Moderate, with Psychotic Episodes associated with Convulsive Disorder, was made." This time, however, the doctors came to a different conclusion. The report continued, "It is felt that he is not psychotic at present, knows right from wrong and is able to cooperate with his counsel in preparing his defense." Furman was returned to jail. No doubt influenced by the second psychiatric report, Mayfield withdrew the insanity plea.

Furman's trial began on September 20, 1968. Chief Assistant Solicitor Robert E. Barker appeared to have overwhelming evidence of guilt. He called Lanell Micke as the first witness. She testified that she and William were the parents of five children. One of the children, Jimmy, was a chronic sleepwalker. Between 2:00 A.M. and 2:30 A.M. on August 11, 1967, she and her husband heard a noise coming from the dining room and kitchen. She thought it was Jimmy sleepwalking, and William got up to investigate.

The prosecutor's questioning continued:

*heard him say "All right, Jimmy, let's go back
to bed." . . . And then all of a sudden I just
heard a real loud sound and he screamed. . . .
I didn't think it was a gun shot. It was just a
real loud sound like somebody had hit him
with something. It was just a real loud crack-
ing sound.*

*Q: Could it have been the sound of a door
closing?*

A: No.

Micke further testified that she did not know
Furman and that she did not know whether he had
entered the house.

Dr. Harold M. Smith testified that he examined
the body of William Micke and described a bullet
wound in the upper chest area that produced "severe
hemorrhage" and death. Dr. Smith extracted the
bullet and turned it over to Detective B. W. Smith.

Fingerprints linked Furman to the Micke house.
The prosecutor questioned Savannah police officer
James Mincey:

*Q. Were you able to find any latent finger-
prints on the back porch of 508 West 63rd
Street?*

A. Yes, Sir.

*Q. What portion of the back porch did you
find the fingerprints?*

*A. There was a washing machine setting
on the back porch under a window.*

*Q. And what did your comparison of
known prints of the defendant, William
Henry Furman, and the latent prints on the
card marked State's Exhibit 10 and 11 show?*

*A. That the right thumb of the known
print and a part of the latent print that came*

Henry Furman, and the latent prints on the card marked State's Exhibit 10 and 11 show?

A. That the right thumb of the known print and a part of the latent print that came off the top of the washing machine were one and the same.

Following the muddy footprints of a person seen fleeing the vicinity of the crime scene, the police had found Furman hiding under his own house at 5020 Temple. Officer Alphonso Hall identified Furman as the same person who emerged from the wooded area near the Micke house and further testified:

Q: Who was under the house?
A: The defendant there.
Q: What did the defendant do, if anything, when you shined your flashlight on him?
A: Well, he was back under the house facing us, you understand, so we told him to come out. And just as we said "come out from under the house" he reached as if he was reaching for his back pocket and I pulled my pistol and I pointed it at him and I told him to come out and don't make any move and I reached my hand to him . . . asked him to take my hand and he reached for my hand. . . . I just pulled him out from under the house.
Q: The person that you pulled out from under the house, is that the same person that you saw emerge from the woods?
A: Yes, sir. . . .
Q: Was a search made of the individual at that time?

Officer J. R. Goode was called as a witness and testified that he searched Furman and found a .22 caliber pistol. Goode testified that the pistol was loaded with six bullets, three of which had been fired.

Detective Smith, who was in charge of the investigation of Micke's murder, testified that he interviewed Furman and advised him of his Miranda rights. One year earlier, the U.S. Supreme Court had ruled in *Miranda v. Arizona* (1966) that police officers must inform suspects of their constitutional rights to remain silent and to have an attorney present during any interrogation.

Smith then testified about Furman's response to the Miranda warning:

Q: And what did he say in regards to wanting an attorney present?

A: He did not want an attorney at that time.

Q: Did the defendant make a statement?
A: Yes.

Q: Was that statement made freely and voluntarily without hope of reward or fear of punishment held out by you and anyone in your presence?

A: That's correct. . . .

Q: Did you then propound your question? . . .

A: I asked him "Did you get in the house?"

Q: What was his answer?

A: He stated "yes," that he got in the kitchen, that the man came in the kitchen, saw him in the kitchen, tried to grab him and when he went out the door the man hit the door, slammed the door between them, he turned around and fired one shot and run.

Finally, Dr. Charles Sullenger of the Georgia State Crime Laboratory testified that he examined the pistol recovered from Furman. The pistol had been test-fired, and the bullet retrieved from the body of William Micke had been fired from the same pistol.

The prosecution appeared to have an airtight case. Furman's only defense seemed to be that Micke's death was accidental and without any intention or malice. Mayfield put his client on the stand, and Furman testified:

> *They got me charged with murder and I admit, I admit going to these folks' home and they did caught me in there and I was coming back out, backing up and there was a wire down there on the floor. I was coming out backwards and fell back and I didn't intend to kill nobody. I didn't know they was behind door. The gun went off and I didn't know nothing about no murder until they arrested me, and when the gun went off I was down on the floor and I got up and ran. That's all [there is] to it.*"

After the prosecution and defense had presented their witnesses and made their closing statements to the jury, Judge Harrison gave lengthy instructions to the jury. He told them about the presumption of innocence, which meant that the prosecution had the burden of proving the defendant guilty beyond a reasonable doubt to the exclusion of every other reasonable explanation. He also told them that if the case rested on circumstantial, or indirect, evidence the proved facts must be consistent with guilt and must exclude every other reasonable explanation. He then instructed the jury on

*Judge Dunbar Harrison of the Chatham County
Superior Court presided at the 1968 murder
trial of William Henry Furman.*

the legal definition of murder—the unlawful killing of a human being, with malice aforethought, express or implied—and the legal definition of involuntary manslaughter—a death not intended but occurring in the commission of an unlawful act. Judge Harrison also instructed the jury on the felony-murder doctrine, which provides that when a death occurs during the perpetration of certain designated felonies, the defendant may be found guilty of first-degree murder—regardless of intent. Burglary is usually designated as one of these felonies. (The felony-murder doctrine is not peculiar to Georgia; most states have enacted the doctrine within their laws.)

He carefully explained the felony-murder doctrine to the jury:

If you believe beyond a reasonable doubt that the defendant broke and entered the dwelling of the deceased with intent to commit a felony or a larceny and that after so breaking and entering with such intent, the defendant killed the deceased in the manner set forth in the indictment, and if you find that such killing was the natural, reasonable and probable consequence of such breaking and entering, then I instruct you that under such circumstances, you would be authorized to convict the defendant of murder and this you would be authorized to do whether the defendant intended to kill the deceased or not.

Finally, Judge Harrison informed the jury that if they found Furman guilty of murder, they were also to decide his sentence. The judge instructed, "I charge you that the punishment [for murder] is death by electrocution but you, the jury, have the

Finally, Judge Harrison informed the jury that if they found Furman guilty of murder, they were also to decide his sentence. The judge instructed, "I charge you that the punishment [for murder] is death by electrocution but you, the jury, have the right in your discretion to recommend him to the mercy of the Court and fix the punishment for life, either of which actions by you would be binding upon the court." Thus, if the jury voted for a verdict that found Furman guilty of murder, it could either give him the death penalty or life imprisonment.

After deliberating for a short period, the jury returned and asked the judge for further guidance:

> *THE JUROR: [There is] among the jurors . . . a difference of opinion on the verdict that we can render. Can we render a verdict, leaving [the punishment] to the discretion of the Court?*
>
> *THE COURT: No, Sir. I have given you the forms of the verdicts. It's up to the jury to decide.*[2]

The jury returned a guilty verdict after deliberating one hour and thirty-five minutes. Although there is no indication on which theory the jury reached its decision, it's a fair assumption that the jury based its decision on the felony-murder doctrine. Furman had attempted to commit a burglary while armed with a pistol. The shooting had taken place during the attempted burglary, and the resulting murder was seemingly a natural and probable consequence of the burglary. The jury did not recommend mercy, thereby sentencing Furman to death. The jury knew nothing about Furman's background or circumstances except that he was twenty-six years old and worked at Superior Upholstery.

for electrocution at such penal institution as may be designated by said Director and the said defendant shall, on November 8, 1969, be put to death by electrocution in the manner provided by law." Furman was then transported from the Chatham County jail to death row at the Georgia State Prison to await execution.

Chapter 2

REACHING THE
SUPREME COURT

Still represented by attorney Mayfield, Furman appealed his conviction and sentence to the Georgia Supreme Court. The procedure to reach the Georgia Supreme Court was relatively routine. Furman filed a notice of appeal following his conviction, and the Chatham County Superior Court in Savannah transmitted copies of relevant court records to the higher court. Trials of serious felonies, such as Furman's, are recorded verbatim by court reporters, who typically use transcribing machines to take down what is said during the case. The verbatim record of Furman's trial was also sent to the Georgia Supreme Court.

After the Georgia Supreme Court received the trial record, Mayfield filed an appellant's brief with the court. The brief is a written argument that sets forth the grounds for appeal with citations of previously reported cases. The prosecution, represented by the Chatham County district attorney and the state attorney general, filed a respondent's brief.

The appeal was then set for oral argument by the Georgia Supreme Court.

In his brief and his oral argument before the Georgia Supreme Court, Mayfield laid out the four major grounds for the appeal:

1. A prospective juror was excluded from the jury because he stated that his opposition to the death penalty would affect his decision as to defendant's guilt. This exclusion was unconstitutional under the Supreme Court's ruling in *Witherspoon v. Illinois* (1968) in which the Court held that exclusion of prospective jurors for reasons that they opposed the death penalty was unconstitutional.
2. The death penalty was cruel and unusual punishment and, therefore, unconstitutional.
3. Furman had not been adequately advised of his constitutional right against self-incrimination after his arrest as required by *Miranda v. Arizona*. Therefore, his fingerprints, confession, and the gun should not have been admitted as evidence.
4. Furman had been arrested on August 11, 1967, and a commitment hearing was held on August 15, more than 48 hours after arrest (in violation of the law).

On April 24, 1969, the Georgia Supreme Court issued a two-page opinion written by Chief Justice Duckworth. The court unanimously rejected all of Mayfield's arguments. Duckworth wrote:

> *A juror having been excluded for cause because he stated that his opposition to the death penalty would affect his decision as to defendant's guilt . . . did not fall within the*

FURMAN v. GEORGIA

*defendant's guilt . . . did not fall within the
rule as laid down in* Witherspoon v. Illinois.
*. . . We find no merit in the contention of
counsel that his constitutional rights had
been violated. . . . We find no violation of*
Miranda v. Arizona *(advice of constitutional
rights), as contended by counsel. . . . The
statutes of this State authorizing capital
punishment have repeatedly been held not to
be cruel and unusual punishment. . . . The
evidence of fingerprints, pistol and admis-
sions which were obtained after his arrest
could be used against him, and no secret
inquisition or interrogation is claimed in
this case.*

Duckworth concluded, "the general grounds of the
motion for new trial are not meritorious."[1]

William Henry Furman, on Georgia's death row,
had one more hope. He could appeal to the U.S.
Supreme Court. After a final decision by the high-
est court in a state, a convicted person has two
means of taking his or her case to the U.S.
Supreme Court. One is to petition a federal district
court for a writ, or order, of habeas corpus.
Guaranteed in Article I, Section 9, of the U.S.
Constitution, a writ of habeas corpus is a procedure
by which a prisoner can test the legality of his arrest
and custody. In his petition, the prisoner alleges
that his confinement is unlawful. The district attorney then files a document known as a return, which
denies that the prisoner is being held in custody
illegally. A hearing takes place, and the federal district court judge studies all the paperwork, asks
questions of the attorneys for each side, and then
either grants or denies the writ. If a writ of habeas
corpus is denied, the prisoner can appeal the deci-

sion through the federal appellate courts, all the way to the Supreme Court.

Prisoners can also appeal their cases directly to the U.S. Supreme Court by filing a petition for a writ of certiorari. Certiorari is a formal writ issued by the Supreme Court to a lower court that requires the transfer of the lower court's records and proceedings in a particular case to the Supreme Court for review. In its rules, the Supreme Court makes it very clear that "Review on a writ of certiorari is not a matter of right but of judicial discretion." Until 1995, a writ of certiorari could be granted "only when there are special and important reasons therefore." The rule was amended in 1995 to provide that a writ would be granted "only for compelling reasons." Before a writ of certiorari can be granted, at least four Supreme Court justices must vote in favor of the Court hearing the appeal.

On behalf of Furman, Mayfield petitioned the U.S. Supreme Court for a writ of certiorari, requesting that the Court review Furman's claim that the death penalty was unconstitutional as cruel and unusual punishment under the Eighth Amendment of the U.S. Constitution. The Eighth Amendment provides: "Excessive bail shall not be required, nor excessive fines imposed, nor cruel and unusual punishments inflicted." Three other petitions for writs of certiorari that claimed the death penalty was cruel and unusual punishment were also pending before the Supreme Court.

In *Branch v. Texas*, the defendant had been convicted of rape and sentenced to death. Elmer Branch had entered the rural home of a sixty-five-year-old widow while she slept and raped her, holding his arm against her throat. As he left, he had told the woman that if she told anyone what had

equivalent of five and a half years of elementary education.

In *Aikens v. California*, the defendant had been convicted of two first-degree murders during the perpetration of rape and was sentenced to death on one murder. Earnest Aikens was under the age of eighteen when he committed the first murder and was sentenced to life imprisonment on that charge.

In *Jackson v. Georgia*, the twenty-one-year-old African-American defendant had been convicted of the rape of a white woman and sentenced to death. A court-appointed psychiatrist said that Lucius Jackson was of average education and average intelligence, not an imbecile or schizophrenic or psychotic, that his traits were the product of environmental influences and that he was competent to stand trial. Jackson had entered the victim's house after her husband left for work, held scissors against the neck of the victim, and demanded money. She could find no money and Jackson raped her with the scissors against her neck. Jackson was a convict who had escaped from a work gang in the area while serving a three-year sentence for auto theft. By coincidence, Judge Dunbar Harrison of the Superior Court of Chatham County had presided over the trials of Lucius Jackson and William Henry Furman.

The U.S. Supreme Court granted certiorari in all four cases, limiting the appeal in each case to the following issue: "Does the imposition and carrying out of the death penalty in [these cases] constitute cruel and unusual punishment in violation of the 8th and 14th Amendments." The Fourteenth Amendment provides that no state can "deprive any person of life, liberty or property, without due process of law." The Fourteenth Amendment's due process clause is important because it gives defen-

any person of life, liberty or property, without due process of law." The Fourteenth Amendment's due process clause is important because it gives defendants in state trials, such as William Henry Furman, additional legal protections beyond what their local state laws provide.

The stage was now set. The U.S. Supreme Court had agreed to hear arguments on the death penalty, an issue of great public concern. Those concerned with law enforcement—including district attorneys, law enforcement officials, and some political conservatives—were optimistic. They had been highly critical of the Supreme Court under the leadership of Chief Justice Earl Warren. During Warren's tenure (1953–69), the Court had expanded the interpretation of Fourteenth Amendment due process rights in a series of cases. In *Mapp v. Ohio* (1961), the Court ruled that evidence recovered through an unlawful search and seizure was not admissible in state courts.[2] This was followed by the controversial *Miranda v. Arizona* (1966), in which a divided Court required that the police advise defendants of their constitutional right against self-incrimination and the right to an attorney before questioning.[3] Many law-enforcement-oriented persons breathed a sigh of relief when Warren retired in 1969. President Richard Nixon appointed Warren Burger as chief justice, and many people thought that he would be more sympathetic to their cause.

People concerned with civil rights were equally hopeful. The National Association for the Advancement of Colored People (NAACP), the American Civil Liberties Union (ACLU), and other liberal groups were encouraged by the Court's grant of certiorari in *Furman* and the other three cases. They had been thrilled by the Supreme Court's decision

Jack Greenberg was serving as chief counsel of the NAACP's Legal Defense and Education Fund (LDF) when Furman v. Georgia *was appealed to the U.S. Supreme Court. The LDF had launched a nation-wide legal attack on capital punishment in 1965.*

in *Witherspoon v. Illinois* (1968), in which it ruled that it was unconstitutional to exclude jurors opposed to the death penalty.[4] They were also heartened by the fact that there had been no executions in the United States since 1967.

William Henry Furman and 669 other prisoners on death rows throughout the United States were also eager for the Court to overturn the death penalty. The Court's decision in *Witherspoon v. Illinois* had recently spared thirty-nine death-row inmates awaiting execution in Illinois. Escaping the death penalty under that ruling was Chicago mass murderer Richard F. Speck, who had brutally murdered eight student nurses in their rooms in 1966. Speck had been sentenced to die in the electric chair.

Pending the decision of the U.S. Supreme Court in *Furman* and the other three cases, all executions were placed on hold. If the Court should rule that execution is cruel and unusual punishment under the Eighth Amendment of the U.S. Constitution, Furman and all other death-row inmates would have their death sentences rescinded, and they would probably receive life sentences. If the U.S. Supreme Court should determine that execution was not cruel and unusual, executions would proceed.

Even if this appeal failed, Furman would still have one last chance of filing a petition for a writ of habeas corpus in federal district court, but that appeal process would probably only prolong his agony on death row. A federal district court might find some violation of fundamental rights, but such an outcome appeared unlikely because the Georgia Supreme Court had found no such violations.

Chapter 3

CAPITAL PUNISHMENT IN HISTORY

To prepare the briefs and oral presentations for their Supreme Court cases, the attorneys representing Furman, Jackson, Aikens, and Branch and the legal staffs of the state attorney general offices of Georgia, California, and Texas researched the history of capital punishment seeking support for their arguments. The attorneys on each side wanted to place the Eighth Amendment's "cruel and unusual" language in its proper historical context.

The words "capital punishment" and "death penalty" are used interchangeably because they describe the same situation: the infliction of death on persons convicted of crimes. The death penalty was a common punishment among most ancient civilizations. Egyptians, Middle Eastern cultures, Persians, Greeks, and Romans all used death as a penalty for certain crimes. The code of Hammurabi, king of Babylon from 2067 to 2025 B.C., provided that the death penalty could be imposed for robbery, adultery, and murder. In the Bible—Exodus, chapter 21—Moses, acting under God's direction, proclaimed the death penalty for murder, striking one's father or mother, reviling or cursing one's mother or father, and kidnapping.

In Europe, the death penalty had become a common punishment for many crimes by the Middle Ages. England, for example, had eight capital offenses by 1500, including treason, petty treason, murder, theft, robbery, burglary, rape, and arson. The number of capital offense crimes soared to 350 by 1780, but by 1819, this number had fallen to about 220.

METHODS OF EXECUTION

The methods of execution have changed through the centuries, but persons in the past have been stoned, burned, drowned, crucified, impaled, strangled, smothered, beheaded, shot, gassed, electrocuted, and injected with drug overdoses. Occasionally, the convicted person has been executed by a different method because of his or her social position. Greek philosopher Socrates, for example, was convicted of corrupting the youth of Athens in 399 B.C. and sentenced to death. He was permitted to drink a beverage made with hemlock, a poisonous herb. The Romans likewise allowed a convicted citizen to take poison, but a convicted slave would be beaten to death. Mary, Queen of Scots, was convicted of plotting to assassinate Queen Elizabeth I of England. She was sentenced to death in 1587. Because of her royal position. Mary was beheaded by sword rather than by ax.

Several execution methods used in the past would certainly be considered cruel and unusual punishment today. Crucifixion was a common execution method in the days of the Roman Empire (27 B.C.–A.D. 476). Depending upon the seriousness of the crime, the accused was either strapped or nailed through the hands and feet to a huge wooden cross. Then the cross was erected in a public place with the person left to die. To expedite death, the accused sometimes had his or her legs broken. The Romans used crucifixion to discourage Jewish rebellion, a typical example being the crucifixion of Jesus Christ. Ironically, the cross of crucifixion became the symbol of Christianity.

Drawing and quartering—killing a condemned criminal by tearing him apart limb from limb—was a popular form of execution centuries ago. Impaling was another dreadful form of capital punishment: condemned persons were stabbed up through their body with a strong lance and then put on display while they died an agonizing death.

Burning at the stake was popular in England, and to some extent, in early America. The condemned was strapped to a post in a public place with wood stacked around the feet. The wood was ignited, and an agonizing and tormenting death followed, often with a crowd of celebrating spectators cheering lustily. French military heroine Joan of Arc, for example, was burned at the stake by the English in 1431. She was nineteen years old.

Public executions were encouraged because of their deterrent effect: spectators were believed to be less likely to commit a serious crime after viewing an execution. Executions also served as a popular entertainment attraction for many people, providing them with a raucous social event and a memorable conversation piece for years to come.

The thousands of public executions during the French Revolution (1789–99) drew huge crowds. The guillotine—a decapitating device named after Joseph Ignace Guillotin—became the official instrument of execution during the bloody Reign of

The manner of the Execution of Colonel James Turner at Lime-street end. Ian. 21. 1663.

A hangman prepares the noose during a 1663 execution in London. Hanging was a popular form of punishment in England.

Terror. The guillotine had a heavy blade that dropped down and sliced off the head of the condemned person. A member of the Constitutional Assembly, Guillotin recommended in 1789 that a uniform method of capital punishment be established so persons condemned to death could be executed quickly and mercifully. The machine itself was designed by Dr. Antoine Louis of the French College of Surgeons and was first used in April 1792. (The guillotine remained the legal method of execution in France until 1981.)

In the United States, hanging became the most popular form of execution. Public executions of condemned criminals before cheering spectators might seem grotesque and repulsive today, but it was once the standard procedure. Particularly in the American West during its early period of settlement, a public hanging day was a time of celebration and recreation. If there was to be a multiple hanging, with two or more prisoners dropping at the same time, folks would attend from miles around. On these special occasions public officials often brought in and paid for a prominent "celebrity" hangman, a man skilled at his job and well known to the people. Up to the day of the hanging, such a man was very popular around town, in demand as a speaker and always welcome as a house guest.

Firing squads have long been common instruments of execution, especially in the military. Executioners armed with rifles line up in a row thirty to forty feet from the condemned person, who is sometimes strapped to a post, and if he or she requests, blindfolded. At the command of "Fire!" the weapons are discharged, and the condemned is killed. To protect the sensibilities of the firing squad members, one or more of the rifles are loaded with blank cartridges. Thus, each individual can rationalize that perhaps it wasn't him or her who killed the condemned person.

Throughout much of history and in many different cultures, various methods of execution were not thought to be cruel. Executions were commonly held in public, and criminals often accepted their punishment without argument. As democratic ideals began to gain widespread support in the eighteenth century, however, people began to question the validity of capital punishment. Movements to abolish or restrict the use of the death penalty began with the writings of French philosophers Baron de Montesquieu (1689–1755) and Voltaire (1694–1778). British philosopher Jeremy Bentham (1748–1832) tried to convince Parliament to reduce the number of death penalty crimes in England.

THE DEATH PENALTY IN AMERICA

By the second half of the eighteenth century, nearly all of the American colonies had adopted most elements of the English legal system, including the death penalty. The Massachusetts Bay Colony, for example, authorized the death penalty for many crimes, including murder, assault, adultery, rape, perjury, idolatry, witchcraft, and blasphemy. The most notorious example of capital punishment in the colonies occurred in Massachusetts in 1692, when a special court in Salem found eighteen men and women guilty of witchcraft and sentenced them to hang. Another suspect was pressed to death for refusing to make a plea after being accused of witchcraft. Twenty years later, the Massachusetts legislature overturned the convictions of all nineteen victims and compensated their families.

Dr. Benjamin Rush (1745–1813), a signer of the Declaration of Independence and surgeon general to the Continental army, is considered the founder of the death penalty abolitionist movement in the

United States. The influential Philadelphian enlisted the support of his friend Benjamin Franklin and prominent Quaker leaders in proposing various prison reforms, including the repeal of the death penalty. Rush argued that the biblical support given capital punishment was questionable and that the threat of hanging did not deter crime.

Rush attracted other Pennsylvanians to his cause, including state attorney general William Bradford. As a result of Rush's reform efforts, Pennsylvania's death penalty was limited to treason and murder, and the Walnut Street Jail in Philadelphia was redesigned, becoming the nation's first penitentiary. In the past, societies had often resorted to the death penalty because of the lack of other types of effective punishment. With the advent of the modern jailhouse, however, punishment by confinement became a viable option.

Rush's proposals attracted followers throughout the nation, but no other states repealed their death penalty laws. Abolitionist societies continued to form along the Atlantic coast, and in 1845, the American Society for the Abolition of Capital Punishment was founded. Horace Greeley, the prominent editor of the *New York Tribune*, became a leading advocate for the abolition of capital punishment. In 1846, Michigan became the first state to abolish the death penalty completely. Rhode Island outlawed the death penalty in 1852, and Wisconsin followed the next year.

Interest in the abolitionist movement declined during the Civil War years. After the war Maine and Iowa abolished the death penalty, but both states soon reinstated it. Maine again abolished the death penalty in 1887. By the 1890s, twenty-one states had changed their laws to allow juries to decide whether death sentences should be applied. Executions did not decline, however, because juries used their discretionary powers to impose the death penalty in most cases.[1] In 1897, Congress reduced the number of federal crimes punishable by death to three: treason, murder, and rape. Between 1907 and 1917, nine states abolished the death penalty, but by 1921 five states had reinstated it.

In the 1920s, noted defense attorney Clarence Darrow led the fight against the death penalty. In a 1924 debate on capital punishment, Darrow summarized a discussion of the statistics on whether the death penalty was a deterrent by observing: "It is a question that cannot be proven one way or the other by statistics. It rests upon things, upon feelings and emotions and arguments much deeper than statistics." Darrow continued, "I know that everybody who is taken into court on a murder charge desires to live, and they do not want to be hanged or electrocuted. Even a thing as alluring as being cooked with electricity doesn't appeal to them."[2]

Darrow fought to prevent the execution of two clients, nineteen-year-old Nathan Leopold, Jr., and eighteen-year-old Richard Loeb, during a 1924 trial that filled newspaper front pages for weeks. The two teenagers pleaded guilty to the thrill killing of fourteen-year-old Robert Franks, but Darrow's eloquent defense got them life terms instead of death sentences.

Law enforcement officials have historically supported capital punishment, but Lewis E. Lawes, the warden at New York's Sing Sing prison, became a leading abolitionist. He spent many hours thinking about his position on the death penalty:

On January 1, 1920, I was appointed warden at Sing Sing, undoubtedly a most difficult prison for an executive officer. I still believed in capital punishment and realized that, under the laws of the State of New York, it

Lewis E. Lawes (left), warden of New York's Sing Sing prison, works in his office with his secretary. Lawes became an outspoken critic of the death penalty and helped found the American League to Abolish Capital Punishment in 1925.

would be necessary for me to assume charge of legal executions. If you, the reader, were directed by name and official title to kill a designated human being, even though the man was a convicted murderer, it would make you pause—and think. It was my duty to determine the day, in fact, the exact hour and minute, death should occur. This gruesome task caused me to seek all obtainable facts relating to capital punishment.

After considerable research and soul-searching, Lawes changed his opinion about capital punishment and helped form the American League to Abolish Capital Punishment in 1925.

Public support for and opposition to capital punishment often fluctuated wildly during the first half of the twentieth century, particularly during high-profile trials. The *Sacco-Vanzetti* case, for example, attracted worldwide attention and bolstered opposition to the death penalty. The defendants, Nicola Sacco and Bartolomeo Vanzetti, were Italian anarchists who were convicted in 1921 for the murders of a paymaster and his guard during a robbery at a shoe factory in South Braintree, Massachusetts. Many observers believed that the two men were innocent but were convicted because of their radical political beliefs. Despite numerous appeals, Sacco and Vanzetti were executed in 1927. Fifty years later, Governor Dukakis of Massachusetts pardoned the two men posthumously.

The kidnapping and murder of the infant son of national hero Charles A. Lindbergh engrossed the nation in 1932 and helped swing the pendulum of public opinion in favor of the death penalty. Bruno Richard Hauptmann was arrested for the crime and convicted in a highly publicized and dramatic trial. Hauptmann was executed in New Jersey's electric chair in April 1936. Hauptmann maintained his innocence to the end, but the evidence seemed overwhelming, although some believed that Hauptmann had not acted alone. The case prompted the passage of the so-called Lindbergh law, which made kidnapping a federal offense when it crossed state lines. Many states passed statutes, called Little Lindbergh laws, that increased the penalties for kidnapping.

After being stalled during World War II, the abolitionist movement gained momentum during the 1950s. The execution of Julius and Ethel Rosenberg in New York's Sing Sing prison in 1953 attracted considerable attention. The Rosenbergs were convicted of conspiring to commit espionage. In the highly publicized trial, Ethel Rosenberg's brother, together with other witnesses, testified that top secret nuclear weapon technology information had been delivered to the Rosenbergs who, in turn, had passed it on to the Soviet Union. As a result, the Soviet Union was able to produce a nuclear bomb much earlier than expected, which significantly threatened domestic security and complicated U.S. foreign policy. The Rosenbergs maintained their innocence to the end, but President Eisenhower turned down requests for clemency. The controversy over their trial and sentence continues today.

Caryl Chessman, the so-called red-light bandit, was convicted of kidnapping in California and sentenced to death. Chessman, who represented himself in a prolonged appeals process, wrote *Cell 2455 Death Row* (1954), a thoughtful and influential book that denounced the death penalty as merely an act of revenge. The death-row author wrote two more books about death row, *Trial by Ordeal* (1955) and *The Face of Justice* (1957), and his case proved to be a catalyst for organizations opposed to capital

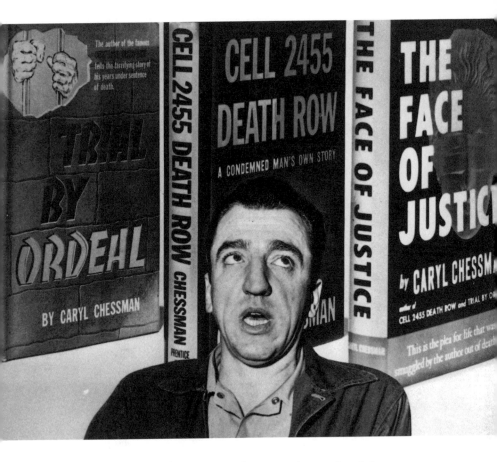

*Caryl Chessman appears here against a backdrop
displaying his three books, which denounced the
death penalty. After appealing his death sentence
for twelve years, Chessman was executed in
California's gas chamber in 1960.*

punishment.[3] Although not responsible for any
deaths, Chessman was executed in California's gas
chamber in 1960.

Opponents of capital punishment soon recognized the enormous difficulty in getting death
penalty laws repealed in each state. They began

41

turning their focus away from state legislatures and toward the courts. Certain organizations, such as the NAACP and the American Civil Liberties Union (ACLU), and many churches and political leaders continued their crusades against the death penalty by seeking to block executions through lawsuits, appeals, and other court actions.

The NAACP's Legal Defense and Education Fund (LDF) was at the forefront of this movement. The LDF was founded in 1939 to litigate civil rights issues and provide legal service to the poor. LDF lawyers repeatedly found themselves defending African-American defendants accused of capital crimes. They had become convinced that the death penalty was unfairly imposed. In 1965, the LDF, under director Jack Greenberg, launched a nationwide legal attack on capital punishment.

These efforts began to bear fruit in 1968, the first year in which no one was put to death in the United States since 1930.[4] The suspension of executions continued through 1972, when *Furman v. Georgia* and its three companion cases reached the Supreme Court. At the time the attorneys in the four cases were honing their arguments, nine states—Alaska, Hawaii, Iowa, Maine, Michigan, Minnesota, Oregon, West Virginia, and Wisconsin—did not have a death penalty. The death penalty was in force for a very few limited crimes, such as treason or murder by a life-term prisoner, in New Mexico, New York, North Dakota, Rhode Island, and Vermont.

Chapter 4

THE LEGAL PRECEDENTS

In addition to researching the history of capital punishment, the attorneys preparing for *Furman* and its three companion cases closely examined the U.S. Constitution and researched earlier Supreme Court cases dealing with death penalty issues. Each side hoped to establish that the weight of the legal precedents supported their position.

The U.S. Constitution, adopted in 1787 and ratified in 1789, established a federal system of government. Under the Constitution, certain governmental powers were delegated to the federal government, such as the power to declare war, make treaties, establish post offices, and coin money. The Tenth Amendment to the Constitution provides that "the powers not delegated to the United States by the Constitution nor prohibited by it to the States, are reserved to the States, respectively, or to the people." Thus, the federal government has delegated powers, and the individual states have residual powers. Questions of which powers are delegated (and, therefore, belonging to the federal government) and which powers are residual (and, therefore, belonging to the states) have resulted in many legal disputes between the federal government and the individual states.

In 1868, following the Civil War, the Fourteenth Amendment was adopted as a means to ensure that the rights of newly freed slaves would be recognized. It prevents states from depriving "any person of life, liberty, or property without due process of law." Although the Fourteenth Amendment was originally drafted to make sure that African-Americans would be afforded protection from state governments, the amendment applies to *all* U.S. citizens, regardless of race. Through an expanded interpretation of the Fourteenth Amendment, the Supreme Court started reviewing state judicial decisions with the focus on whether they violated any fundamental right guaranteed by the U.S. Constitution and its amendments. Although the Court has not incorporated, or applied, all of the Bill of Rights guarantees to state court proceedings, it has ruled that certain guarantees listed in the first ten amendments cannot be ignored by the states. The fundamental rights of a criminal defendant guaranteed by the federal constitution now include such basic protections as the privilege against self-incrimination, the exclusion of a confession obtained by coercion, the right to counsel at trial, and the right to a jury trial.

Because most crimes punishable by death originate in state courts, the Fourteenth Amendment's due process clause has emerged as an important tool in death penalty cases. The first major death penalty case that dealt with the due process clause and a review of a state court decision was *Powell v. Alabama*. In *Powell*, nine young African Americans, including Ozie Powell, had been accused of raping two white women. The trial judge had asked local lawyers to volunteer to represent the defendants, but not one had stepped forward. On the day of the trial, the judge had appointed an attorney to defend the nine young men, who became known as the Scottsboro Boys. Although doctors who had examined the women after the alleged rape testified that no rape had occurred, all of the young men—except the youngest, who was thirteen years old—had been convicted and sentenced to death. Acting under the authority of the Fourteenth Amendment, the Supreme Court in *Powell v. Alabama* (1932) ruled that an accused in a death penalty case "requires the guiding hand of counsel at every step in the proceedings against him."[1]

The *Powell* decision guaranteed that a defendant charged with a death penalty offense could obtain both the legal advice necessary to identify the grounds for appeals and the assistance necessary to carry such appeals forward. Every defendant charged with any crime punishable by death was guaranteed an attorney. Defendants unable to afford their own attorneys would be appointed one. Today, in counties that have a public defender's office, a deputy public defender is normally appointed for poor defendants. When the county does not have a public defender, individual attorneys are appointed for indigent defendants. The appointed attorneys normally receive some monetary compensation from the county.

For many years, the Supreme Court refused to apply the Eighth Amendment—which provides that "excessive bail shall not be required, nor excessive fines imposed, nor cruel and unusual punishments inflicted"—to state court proceedings. The first important case dealing with the Eighth

Amendment's cruel and unusual punishment clause was *Wilkerson v. Utah* (1879). Utah was a territory of the United States at the time, but legislative power was given to a governor and a legislative assembly. Acting under that authority, the Utah Territory enacted a law providing that any person who was convicted and sentenced to death should suffer death by being "shot, hanged or beheaded as the court may direct." Wallace Wilkerson was found guilty of murder, and the judge ordered that he be executed by a firing squad. The Supreme Court upheld the judge's order, ruling that execution by firing squad was not cruel and unusual punishment.[2]

In *In re Kemmler* (1890), the Supreme Court upheld electrocution as a permissible method of execution. Two years earlier, New York had authorized the use of the electric chair for executions, and William Kemmler became the first person sentenced to die in the device. In the course of its opinion, the Court conceded that electrocution was "unusual" because it was a new invention, but the Court determined that it was an instantaneous and "painless" death. The Court decided this case on the basis of the Fourteenth Amendment's due process clause but stated in its opinion that the Eighth Amendment was not applicable to the states.[3]

In 1892, the Supreme Court heard the case of *O'Neil v. Vermont*. John O'Neil had been convicted of 307 counts of unlawful sale of liquor. He was fined $6,140 plus court costs of $497.96 and sentenced to jail until the fine and costs were paid. If the fine and costs were not paid by a certain date, O'Neil was to be sentenced to about fifty-four years at hard labor. The Court ruled by a vote of 6–3 that the Eighth Amendment was not applicable to the states. O'Neil's plea for mercy was denied.[4]

The electric chair at Sing Sing prison was captured in this 1930s photograph. In In re Kemmler *(1890), the Supreme Court ruled that execution by electrocution was not a cruel and unusual method of punishment.*

In *Weems v. United States* (1910), an officer in the Coast Guard of the U.S. Government of the Philippine Islands was convicted of falsifying a public and official document. Paul Weems was sentenced to fifteen years incarceration at hard labor with chains on his ankles, to an unusual loss of his civil rights, and to perpetual surveillance. The Supreme Court determined that this sentence was cruel and unusual punishment.[5]

In *Louisiana ex rel. Francis v. Resweber* (1947), the fifteen-year-old defendant had been convicted of murder and sentenced to die in the electric chair. He was strapped in the device, and the executioner threw the switch. Nothing happened because of some mechanical failure. Willie Francis was removed from the electric chair and returned to death row. A new death warrant was issued by the governor of Louisiana for a second effort. Francis claimed double jeopardy along with other legal complaints. The Supreme Court in a 5–4 decision determined that Louisiana could execute Francis.[6] It did.

In *Trop v. Dulles* (1958) a lower court had ruled that a native-born American had lost his citizenship by reason of conviction by court-martial for wartime desertion. While serving in the U.S. Army in French Morocco in 1944, Albert Trop escaped from a stockade where he had been confined following a breach of discipline. The following day he willingly surrendered to an army officer and was returned to the stockade. Trop received a general court-martial, was convicted of wartime desertion, and was sentenced to three years at hard labor with a forfeiture of all pay. He received a dishonorable discharge from the army. When Trop applied for a passport in 1952, his application was denied on grounds that he had lost his citizenship by reason of his dishonorable discharge for wartime desertion. Chief Justice Earl Warren wrote the majority opinion in a 5–4 decision that found the Nationality Act of 1940 partially unconstitutional and also ruled that loss of citizenship is a cruel and unusual punishment barred by the Eighth Amendment. In his opinion, Warren pointed out that the Court had recognized in *Weems* that the words of the Eighth Amendment "are not precise and that their scope is not static. The Amendment must draw its meaning from the evolving standards of decency that mark the progress of a maturing society."[7]

In *Robinson v. California* (1962), the Supreme Court reviewed a California law that required a minimum ninety-day sentence for anyone convicted of being "addicted to marijuana." The Court ruled that the ninety-day-sentence law was cruel and unusual punishment in violation of the Eighth Amendment. It reasoned that addiction is a disease rather than a crime. Because prosecution for addiction cannot be justified, the Court struck down the statute, ruling that it was unconstitutional.[8]

The Supreme Court considered a similar statute in *Powell v. Texas* (1968). Leroy Powell was convicted and fined twenty dollars for violating a Texas statute that outlawed drunkenness in a public place. The Court approved this sentence by a 5–4 vote, ruling that unlike the defendant in *Robinson v. California*, Powell had become drunk by his own volitional act.[9]

The Supreme Court first encountered the argument that the death penalty was cruel and unusual punishment in the case of *Rudolph v. Alabama* (1963). The petitioner had been sentenced to death for rape and filed a petition for a writ of certiorari with the U.S. Supreme Court requesting that his sentence be reviewed by the high court. The petition was denied, but Justice Arthur Goldberg, joined by Justice William Douglas and Justice William Brennan, dissented from the majority's denial of the petition, writing:

I would grant certiorari in this case . . . to consider whether the Eighth and Fourteenth Amendments to the United States Con-

stitution permit the imposition of the death penalty on a convicted rapist who has neither taken nor endangered human life. The following questions . . . seem relevant and worthy of argument and consideration. (1) In light of the trend both in this country and throughout the world against punishing rape by death, does the imposition of the death penalty by those States which retain it for rape violate "evolving standards of decency that mark the progress of maturing society" or "standards of decency more or less universally accepted?" (2) Is the taking of human life to protect a value other than human life consistent with the constitutional proscription against "punishments which by their excessive . . . severity are greatly disproportioned to the offense?" (3) Can the permissible aims of punishment (e.g., deterrence, isolation, rehabilitation) be achieved as effectively by punishing rape less severely than by death (e.g. by life imprisonment); if so, does the imposition of the death penalty for rape constitute "unnecessary cruelty?"[10]

In *McGautha v. California* (1971), the Supreme Court reviewed a California statute governing the imposition of the death penalty. Dennis McGautha had been convicted of murder. Under California law, if a person was found guilty of first-degree murder, a second penalty trial was held before the same jury, and evidence relating to penalty would be introduced by the defendant and the state. The jury decided on a sentence of either life imprisonment or death during the penalty trial. A companion case, *Crampton v. Ohio* (1971), involved an Ohio law similar to the California statute. A jury found

James Crampton guilty and determined his sentence in a single trial.

The Supreme Court granted certiorari to determine whether either defendant's constitutional rights were infringed by permitting the jury to impose the death penalty without any governing standards. Besides appointed counsel for each defendant, Jack Greenberg, James M. Nabritt III, Michael Meltsner of Columbia Law school, and Anthony Amsterdam of Stanford Law School appeared as amici curiae (a Latin phrase meaning "friends of the court") in support of McGautha and Crampton.

In *McGautha*, the trial judge had instructed the jury: "Notwithstanding facts, if any, proved in mitigation or aggravation, in determining which punishment shall be inflicted, you are entirely free to act according to your own judgment, conscience, and absolute discretion. That verdict must express the individual opinion of each juror."[11] In *Crampton*, the jury had been instructed, "If you find the defendant guilty of murder in the first degree, the punishment is death, unless you recommend mercy, in which event the punishment is imprisonment in the penitentiary during life."[12]

The lawyers for McGautha and Crampton claimed that the absence of standards to guide the jury's discretion on their clients' punishment was unconstitutional. They argued that to leave a jury completely at large to impose or withhold the death penalty as it sees fit violates the basic guarantees of the Fourteenth Amendment's due process clause. Justice John Harlan wrote the Court's opinion, which rejected the claims of McGautha and Crampton. He concluded, "The procedures which petitioners challenge are those by which most capital trials in this country are conducted and by which all were conducted until a few years ago." Although the Court decided the case without addressing the basic constitutional issue of whether the death penalty was cruel and unusual punishment, in a concurring opinion Justice Hugo Black stated emphatically, "The 8th Amendment forbids 'cruel and unusual punishments.' In my view, these words cannot be read to outlaw capital punishment because that penalty was in common use and authorized by law here and in the countries from which our ancestors came at the time the Amendment was adopted."

Justice Douglas, joined by Justice Brennan and Justice Thurgood Marshall, wrote a lengthy dissenting opinion, which concluded that the laws of California and Ohio were unconstitutional because they provided no criteria by which a jury could determine the penalty of life or death.

Justices Black and Harlan retired shortly after this decision and were replaced by two justices, Lewis Powell and William Rehnquist, appointed by President Richard M. Nixon. When certiorari was granted in *Furman* and its companion cases, the lawyers and justices supporting the death penalty probably felt confident that Furman would be decided in accordance with McGautha. The vote in the *McGautha* case had been 6–3. The observers of the Supreme Court probably assumed there would be no drastic change as Furman came up for decision. It would probably be just another 6–3 vote.

Chapter 5

THE COURT DECIDES

After the U.S. Supreme Court grants a writ of certiorari, it is customary procedure for all interested parties to file briefs. A brief submitted to the Supreme Court must be in booklet form and is limited to 50 pages if single-spaced and 110 pages if double-spaced. A brief usually contains an introduction, which defines the precise legal question to be decided by the Court; a summary of the case; a summarized argument with paragraph headings; and a formal request for a specific action. The case is then set for oral argument before all nine members of the Court. The chief justice presides over the oral argument, which takes place in the setting of the Supreme Court's formal courtroom.

After argument, the justices take the case under advisement. They typically discuss the case through meetings and written proposals. After the case is decided in a closed meeting, one of the justices is designated to write the opinion. The opinion is then approved by the justices and adopted as the opinion of the Court.

Strict secrecy is observed throughout the internal proceedings of the Supreme Court. A formal public meeting is then held at which the opinion is announced. Traditionally the justice who writes the majority opinion will read the opinion from the bench to the public gathered in the hearing room. This practice has generally changed in recent years; one justice now gives a short explanation of the decision from the bench. There are many variations of this procedure, which may include the reading of dissenting opinions.

THE *FURMAN* BRIEFS

The procedure was no different for the four death penalty cases before the court in 1972. Lawyers for all the parties involved filed briefs in the *Furman, Aikens, Jackson,* and *Branch* cases. In its writ of certiorari, the Court had limited the issue that it would consider on appeal to one question: "Does the imposition and carrying out of the death penalty in [these cases] constitute cruel and unusual punishment in violation of the Eighth and Fourteenth Amendments?"

Several attorneys participated in the preparation of the brief for *Furman v. Georgia*, including B. Clarence Mayfield, Furman's original trial attorney; Michael Meltsner of Columbia Law School; and Anthony G. Amsterdam of Stanford Law School. Their brief's summary of argument was that: "1. Petitioner's sentence of death is a rare, random and arbitrary infliction, prohibited by the 8th amendment; and 2. The 8th amendment forbids affirmance of a death sentence upon this record, which casts doubt upon petitioner's mental soundness. To relegate petitioner to the torments and vicissitudes of a death sentence without appropriate inquiry into his mental condition is to subject him to cruel and unusual punishment."

The brief went on to emphasize Furman's mental condition. The trial record included Furman's referral to the Georgia Central State Hospital for a psychiatric evaluation pending trial. The brief stated:

> *Petitioner was diagnosed on February 28, 1968, to be afflicted with "Mental Deficiency, Mild to Moderate, with Psychotic Episodes associated with Convulsive Disorder," and was found incapable of cooperating with counsel in his defense. Although this latter incapacity was found no longer to exist on April 15, 1968, the same diagnosis was reported. Petitioner was not found to be psychotic; and the character and extent of his condition are not otherwise disclosed; but the record at the least reveals grounds for the gravest doubt of his mental stability. . . . For any man, be he mentally firm or infirm, condemnation under a sentence of death and "the Thousand Days" on death row create conditions of mind-twisting stress. . . . Modern techniques of execution have aimed at minimizing the physical pain of dying. But these modern techniques have retained to the fullest the exquisite psychological suffering of the condemned man. . . . Institutional practices on death row recognize the likelihood of extreme reactions from the condemned, particularly suicide attempts. . . . The cheating of the chair by escape or suicide is rendered practically impossible by . . . extraordinary precautions against these contingencies. . . . Under these circumstances,*

we believe that a judgment inflicting a sentence of death upon petitioner, in the absence of further inquiries into his mental state, subjects him to cruel and unusual punishment. . . . These torments are agonizing even for a mind of normal stability, but may be unbearable for an unstable man. . . . Without adequate judicial inquiry into the mental state of the defendant, a death penalty may be tantamount to a sentence of insanity.[1]

The respondents—the states of Georgia, Texas, and California—were represented by attorneys from their respective state attorneys general offices. Their briefs argued precedent: a long series of cases decided by the U.S. Supreme Court had held that the death penalty did not constitute cruel and unusual punishment. The briefs of the respondents also contained references to Supreme Court cases that discussed standards by which to judge cruel and unusual punishments. These included punishment by torture, excessive punishment for the crime involved, and punishment that was "unconscionable" and "shocking to the conscience of reasonable men."

The respondents' brief asserted:

The death penalty is more appropriate for a maturing society: as the society becomes more enlightened, so greater becomes the breach between murder and rape on the one hand and responsible conduct by its members on the other. Thus, the imposition of the death penalty in appropriate cases: 1. Enhances the dignity of men (the criminal, the society, and the victim); 2. Places a greater gap between violent crime and what is expected of the

*responsible citizen; 3. Demands greater safe-
guards to assure it is arrived at by due
process; and 4. Expresses society's utter con-
demnation of capital crimes. . . . To be strick-
en as unconstitutional, the death penalty
must be so cruel and unusual that it deprives
a State prisoner of due process of law; it
must be so cruel and unusual that it exceeds
the outer boundaries beyond which State legislatures may not travel; it must be so cruel
and unusual that, regardless of the enormity
of the crimes sought to be punished and cur-
tailed, it cannot be considered by the State
Legislature. . . . The death penalty does not
approach that fine line, because it is not
inhuman to deprive one of life as a consequence of his own anti-social, voluntary
behavior, because it is not barbarous (uncivi-
lized); "mercilessly harsh or cruel"; "offending
against contemporary standards of correct-
ness"; Nor is it torturous [inflicting intense
pain]. . . . Nor is it so disproportionate to the
gravity or enormity of the crime. . . . Nor was
it arrived at in the manner so lacking in due
process. . . . Nor is it cruel and unusual punishment of what is sought to be accomplished.
Nor is it cruel, disposed to inflict pain, caus-
ing or conducive to injury, grief or pain.*

*Petitioners argue that the death penalty
is meted out arbitrarily and discriminatorily
to Negroes. But it must be remembered that
both Furman and Jackson were tried in the
latter months of 1968 after the Georgia jury
selection system was corrected to expunge the
element of prima facie discrimination which
arose from the use of segregated tax digest as
a source of jurors by substituting the voter*

*lists. The potentiality of racially discrimina-
tory juries was erased in both of these cases.*[2]

The brief also pointed out the drastic effect of
declaring the death penalty unconstitutional.

In addition to the briefs of the petitioners and
respondents in the four death penalty cases, the
Supreme Court reviewed briefs submitted by other
parties. In cases involving important legal issues,
such as *Furman v. Georgia*, groups representing
many different viewpoints provide their expertise
and opinions to the Court by submitting amicus
curiae briefs supporting one of the parties in the
case. (Seeking to avoid being overwhelmed by amicus briefs, the Court requires that amicus curiae
briefs be filed only with the consent of all parties to
the case.)

Many amicus curiae briefs were filed in
Furman, including those by the State of Alaska, the
State of Indiana, the National Council of the
Churches of Christ, the Synagogue Council of
America, the West Virginia Council of Churches,
the Committee of Psychiatrists for Evaluation of
the Death Penalty, the American Civil Liberties
Union, the National Association for the Advance-
ment of Colored People, the National Legal Aid and
Defender Association, and even one by a number
of governors.

An amicus curiae brief in support of the petitioners was filed by former prison officials, including Clinton Duffy, a former warden at California's
San Quentin prison. The brief argued that the
death penalty is arbitrarily and capriciously
imposed: "What is it that distinguishes those who
have been condemned to die from those who are
permitted to live? . . . Bluntly, the distinguishing
characteristics are poverty, ignorance, and out of all

statistical proportion, race." The brief went on to show that Duffy had made exhaustive personal efforts to determine what impact the death penalty had had on convicted criminals. Based on his research, Duffy concluded that "the criminal has acted either out of passion or with the unalterable belief that he will not be caught." The brief of the prison officials concluded: "The death penalty is barbaric," and then went on to describe the procedural details that accompany an execution.

The brief of the Committee of Psychiatrists for Evaluation of the Death Penalty argued that the death penalty:

> *constitutes cruel and unusual punishment because of the psychological torture which it inflicts. . . . A good many of these doomed men end up in the hands of the psychiatrist. The strain of existence on Death Row is very likely to produce behavioral aberrations ranging from malingering to acute psychotic breaks. . . . The prisoners who escape psychosis frequently experience other reactions to the stress of impending death: insomnia, withdrawal, depression, paranoia, obsessive rumination, anxiety and delusions. The damage is increased by the steadily lengthening time which prisoners spend on death row. . . . The legitimate government interests in the punishment of criminals are (1) rehabilitation, (2) isolation, and (3) deterrence. . . . No study has yet shown that capital punishment deters crime.*[3]

The brief of the National Legal Aid and Defender Association pointed out that the "Eighth Amendment prohibition against cruel and unusual punishment was a dynamic concept depending upon the evolving standards of decency that mark the progress of a maturing society . . . at the time of the adoption of the Eighth Amendment capital punishment was practiced in colonial America. . . . Our notions of what constitutes cruel and unusual punishment have undergone significant changes . . . a punishment is cruel and unusual if it goes beyond what is necessary to achieve a legitimate penal interest."

A brief was filed jointly by the NAACP, the National Urban League, the Southern Christian Leadership Conference, the Mexican-American Legal Defendant and Educational Fund, and the National Council of Negro Women. This consolidated brief asserted that a disproportionate number of minority defendants had been executed between 1930 and 1967, a period when African-Americans constituted roughly 10 percent of the population. The brief presented the following statistics—which show the number of persons executed for a particular offense and the percentage of those convicted of the crime who were executed—to support their argument:

Offense	Black	White	Other	Total
Rape	405 (89.0%)	48 (10.6%)	2 (0.4%)	455
Murder	1630 (48.9%)	1665 (49.9%)	40 (1.2%)	3,335
Other	31 (44.3%)	39 (55.7%)	0	70[4]

A group of past and current state governors also filed an amicus curiae brief. This group included former governors Edmund "Pat" Brown of California, David Cargo of New Mexico, Elbert Carvel of Delaware, Michael DiSalle of Ohio, Philip Hoff of Vermont, Theodore McKeldin of Maryland, and Endicott Peabody of Massachusetts. Two current governors, Milton J. Shapp of Pennsylvania and Grant Sawyer of Nevada, also joined the brief. This brief pointed out that state governors had personal experience in judging the death penalty because the condemned person usually asks a governor to commute his or her sentence to life imprisonment as an act of mercy. A governor is frequently the only person standing between the condemned person and the execution chamber, the last person to make the decision between life and death.

The governors asked the Supreme Court to declare the death penalty unconstitutional as cruel and unusual. "Generally, the people who sit in death row waiting to know whether the Governor will permit them to live or to die, follow a uniform pattern," the brief argued. "They are men and women who generally have not had the finances necessary to enlist the services of the peculiarly talented counsel. . . . They are generally unschooled, often illiterate, many times mentally inadequate and frequently the result of local hysteria which cries for a vengeance. . . . Not until one has watched the hands of a clock marking the last minutes of a condemned man's existence, knowing that he alone has the temporary godlike power to stop the clock, can he realize the agony of deciding an appeal for executive clemency."

The State of Alaska, which did not have the death penalty, filed an amicus curiae brief urging the Supreme Court to find the death penalty unconstitutional employing a subjective test of "evolving standards of decency that mark the progress of maturing society" as enunciated by the Supreme Court in *Trop v. Dulles* in 1958. The State of Indiana urged that the Supreme Court approve the death penalty and its existing procedure.

THE JUSTICES

Richard Nixon, who was president in 1972 when *Furman* was decided, supported the death penalty. He had appointed four of the justices who heard *Furman*: Chief Justice Warren E. Burger and associate justices Harry A. Blackmun, Lewis F. Powell, and William H. Rehnquist. The other five associate justices had been appointed by different presidents: William O. Douglas by Franklin D. Roosevelt, William J. Brennan and Potter Stewart by Dwight D. Eisenhower, Byron R. White by John F. Kennedy, and Thurgood Marshall by Lyndon B. Johnson.

Labels of "liberal" or "conservative" are often misleading when describing U.S. Supreme Court justices. They are appointed for life to ensure their independence, and several justices have made decisions that upset the presidents who appointed them. Supreme Court justices are usually categorized either as supporters of judicial restraint or as supporters of judicial activism. Justices who favor judicial restraint prefer to follow precedents, believing that the Court generally should not reverse or modify judicial decisions that have been made in the past. These justices tend to interpret the Constitution narrowly, basing their judgments on what they believe the Founding Fathers intended when they wrote the Constitution. They maintain that the Supreme Court is neither a lawmaker nor a policy setter. Justices Rehnquist and Powell, for example, have been characterized as supporters of judicial restraint. Justices who take an activist approach, however, believe that the Supreme Court should not be constrained by traditions and precedents. These justices believe the Constitution is a living document that is flexible enough to meet the new challenges of our modern world. The Court, they assert, should play an important role in

President Richard M. Nixon, a supporter of capital punishment, had appointed four of the nine Supreme Court justices who heard Furman v. Georgia.

helping bring about political and social change. Justices Douglas, Brennan, and Marshall have been widely considered supporters of the concept of judicial activism.

In framing the arguments that they would present to the Court, the lawyers involved in *Furman, Branch, Jackson,* and *Aiken* looked closely at the individual justices who would be deciding the case. Although Supreme Court justices are impartial interpreters of the law, at least in theory, they're also human. They have different theories about judicial decision making, different approaches to their duties, and different personal experiences that may have some effect on the way that they vote on a particular issue.

Warren Burger was born in St. Paul, Minnesota and grew up in modest circumstances. He took extension courses at the University of Minnesota for two years and attended a night law school. Combining study with work as a life insurance salesman, he earned his law degree from St. Paul College of Law in 1931. He practiced law in St. Paul and became active in the Republican party. He attended the 1952 Republican Convention and helped Eisenhower win the presidential nomination. Burger was appointed head of the Justice Department's Civil Division, where he supervised 180 attorneys, and in 1959 he was appointed judge of the U.S. Court of Appeals for the District of Columbia. Burger served on that court until Nixon appointed him as chief justice in 1969.

William Douglas, who had served on the high court for thirty-three years when *Furman* was argued, was born in Minnesota in 1898. His father was a Presbyterian minister who eventually settled the family in Yakima, Washington. Douglas graduated from Whitman College, where he was student body president, participated on the debating team, and was elected to Phi Beta Kappa. He graduated second in his class from Columbia University Law School and joined a Wall Street law firm. After several years of law practice, he became a professor at Yale Law School. In 1936, he was appointed a member of the Securities and Exchange Commission in Washington, D.C. Three years later, President Franklin Roosevelt appointed Douglas to the U.S. Supreme Court.

William Brennan was born in New Jersey in 1906. He graduated with high honors from the University of Pennsylvania and was a scholarship student at Harvard Law School. He was serving on the New Jersey Supreme Court when President Eisenhower appointed him to the U.S. Supreme Court in 1956. Throughout his tenure, Brennan tended to be a civil libertarian.

Potter Stewart was born in Michigan in 1915. After graduating from Yale and Cambridge, he practiced law in New York City and Cincinnati, where he served on the city council and as vice mayor. In 1954, he was appointed to the U.S. Court of Appeals and in 1958, Eisenhower appointed him to the U.S. Supreme Court.

Byron White was born in Colorado in 1917. Nicknamed "Whizzer," White became an all-American running back for the University of Colorado's football team. After graduation and election to Phi Beta Kappa, White accepted a Rhodes scholarship to study at Oxford in England. He also played professional football with the Detroit Lions. After Oxford, White attended Yale Law School until World War II. During World War II, White was a naval intelligence officer in the South Pacific, where he became acquainted with John Kennedy. After the war, White graduated from Yale Law School and

The Supreme Court poses for a photograph in 1972, the year it decided Furman v. Georgia. *The justices are: (seated, left to right) Potter Stewart, William Douglas, Warren Burger, William Brennan, Byron White, and (standing, left to right) Lewis Powell, Thurgood Marshall, Harry Blackmun, and William Rehnquist.*

served as a law clerk to Fred Vinson, chief justice of the U.S. Supreme Court. Returning to Colorado to practice law, White became involved in John Kennedy's presidential campaign in 1960. In 1962, President Kennedy appointed White to the Supreme Court.

Thurgood Marshall grew up in Baltimore. He attended Lincoln University, graduating cum laude, and then enrolled at Howard University Law School, where he also graduated with honors. Passing the Maryland bar in 1933, Marshall practiced law in Baltimore, where he became attorney for the local chapter of the NAACP. Taking a job with the NAACP's Legal Defense and Education Fund, Marshall became one of the nation's outstanding civil rights attorneys. John Kennedy appointed Marshall to the U.S. Court of Appeals in 1962. Three years later, Marshall was appointed by President Johnson as Solicitor General and then to the Supreme Court in 1967.

Harry Blackmun grew up in St. Paul, Minnesota, and was a classmate and personal friend of Chief Justice Burger. He graduated from Harvard University and Harvard Law School. He served as a law clerk to a U.S. Circuit Court judge. He taught at St. Paul College of Law and in 1945 began teaching part-time at the University of Minnesota Law School while serving as resident counsel of the Mayo Clinic. Dwight Eisenhower appointed him as U.S. Circuit Court judge, a position that he held until President Nixon appointed him to the U.S. Supreme Court in 1970.

Lewis Powell, along with Justice Rehnquist the newest member of the Court, was born in Virginia and graduated from Washington & Lee College and Harvard Law School. He practiced law in Richmond, Virginia, and eventually became a partner in a prestigious law firm, where he gained national recognition as a corporate lawyer. Powell eventually served on the board of directors of eleven major companies and became a leader among attorneys, serving as president of the American Bar Association, the American College of

Trial Lawyers, and the American Bar Foundation, and as vice president of the National Legal Aid and Defender Association. He was appointed to the U.S. Supreme Court in 1971 by President Nixon.

William Rehnquist, a native of Milwaukee, Wisconsin, attended Stanford University, majoring in political science and graduating Phi Beta Kappa. Rehnquist received master's degrees from Stanford and Harvard before enrolling at Stanford Law School, where he graduated first in his class. He served as clerk to U.S. Supreme Court Justice Robert Jackson and then settled in Phoenix, Arizona, to practice law. He became active in the Republican party, serving as state chairman and as national field director for the presidential campaigns of Barry Goldwater in 1964 and Richard Nixon in 1968. In 1968, he was appointed assistant U.S. attorney general. In 1971, Nixon appointed Rehnquist to the U.S. Supreme Court. (In 1986, Ronald Reagan would appoint him as chief justice.)

ORAL ARGUMENTS AND THE DECISION

In January 1972, *Time* magazine described the upcoming Supreme Court hearing on *Furman v. Georgia* as focused on the question, "Has the U.S. reached the point at which the death penalty affronts the basic standards of decency of contemporary society?" The article singled out Stanford law professor Anthony G. Amsterdam as "the principal architect of the abolition campaign." The article went on to report that Amsterdam "has developed an intricate argument. He finds that execution is now generally reserved for a few socially unacceptable, personally ugly and invariably poor defendants; a disproportionate number are from minority groups. 'If a penalty is generally, fairly and uniformly enforced,' says Amsterdam, 'then it will be thrown off the books as soon as the public can no longer accept it. But when the penalty is enforced for a discriminatory selected few, then all the pressures which normally exist to strike an indecent penalty off the books no longer exist. The short of the matter is that when a penalty is so barbaric that it can gain public acceptance only by being rarely, arbitrarily and discriminatorily enforced, it plainly affronts the general standards of decency of the society.' "[5]

The *Furman, Jackson, Branch*, and *Aikens* cases were argued before the Supreme Court on January 17, 1972. Anthony Amsterdam argued on behalf of William Henry Furman, and individual attorneys argued for the other defendants and for the respondents. The Supreme Court took *Furman* and its companion cases under advisement with no suggestions during oral argument as to how they would rule. Death penalty abolitionists had presented their best possible case, but the weight of legal precedent favored a continuation of the death penalty.

While *Furman* and its companion cases were pending decision, the California Supreme Court burst into the limelight with its surprising decision in *People v. Anderson*. In a 6–1 decision, the California Supreme Court struck down California's death penalty statute.[6] The language of the California Constitution differed from that in the U.S. Constitution: it prohibited "cruel *or* unusual" punishment, whereas the federal constitution prohibited "cruel *and* unusual" punishment. Because of the *Anderson* decision, Earnest Aikens, a defendant in one of the cases being considered along with *Furman*, escaped the death sentence, and the U.S. Supreme Court eliminated his case from consideration. More than one hundred other death-row inmates escaped the death penalty in California, including murderer Charles Manson and Sirhan Sirhan, the assassin of Senator Robert Kennedy. California governor Ronald Reagan, a death penalty supporter, was clearly upset with the decision because he had appointed Donald Wright, who wrote the *Anderson* opinion, as chief justice of the California Supreme Court.

The U.S. Supreme Court handed down its decision on the *Furman, Jackson,* and *Branch* cases on June 29, 1972. Its 233-page decision encompassed all three cases and is generally referred to as *Furman v. Georgia.* The Court's per curiam decision ruled that the "imposition and carrying out of the death penalty in these cases constitutes cruel and unusual punishment. . . . The judgment in each case is therefore reversed insofar as it leaves undisturbed the death sentence imposed, and the cases are remanded for further proceedings." (A per curiam opinion is an opinion of the Court that is authored by the whole court rather than by a particular justice; *per curiam* is a Latin phrase meaning "by the court.")

In effect, *Furman* was decided by a 5–4 vote, but each justice wrote a separate opinion, so there was a total of nine separate opinions in the case. The nine opinions discuss every conceivable argument for and against the death penalty and its application. Justices Douglas, Brennan, Stewart, White, and Marshall voted in favor of the per curiam judgment, but each filed a separate opinion. Chief Justice Burger and justices Blackmun, Powell, and Rehnquist voted against the per curiam judgment, and each filed a separate dissenting opinion.

The per curiam opinion drew a fine line. It did not state that the death penalty was cruel and unusual but that "the *imposition and carrying out*

*Justice William Brennan took an absolute
position—that the death sentence is always
unconstitutional under the Eighth Amendment—
in his separate opinion in* Furman v. Georgia.

of the death penalty . . . constitutes cruel and unusual punishment." It was only the procedures in the cases before the Court that were cruel and unusual, not the penalty itself.

Justices Brennan took an absolute position, viewing capital punishment itself as cruel and unusual. He asserted that a death sentence is always unconstitutional under the Eighth Amendment. After reviewing the constitutional history of the Eighth Amendment, Brennan wrote:

> *A punishment is cruel and unusual, therefore, if it does not comport with human dignity. . . . Punishment must not by its severity be degrading to human dignity. . . . Death is a unique punishment in the United States. . . . Death is today an unusually severe punishment, unusual in its pain, in its finality, and in its enormity. No other existing punishment is comparable to death in terms of physical and mental suffering. . . . There is, then, no substantial reason to believe that the punishment of death, as currently administered, is necessary for the protection of society. . . . Today, death is a uniquely and unusually severe punishment. When examined by the principles applicable under the cruel and unusual punishments clause, death stands condemned as fatally offensive to human dignity. The punishment of death is therefore "cruel and unusual" and the states may not inflict it as a punishment for crimes.*[7]

Justice Marshall filed a long, detailed opinion in which he asserted, like Brennan, that capital punishment was cruel and unusual. He stated:

Perhaps the most important principle in analyzing cruel and unusual punishment questions is one that is reiterated again and again in the prior opinions of the court: i.e., that cruel and unusual language must draw its meaning from the evolving standards of decency that mark the progress of a maturing society. Thus a penalty that was permissible at one time in our nation's history is not necessarily permissible today. . . . There is but one conclusion that can be drawn from all of this—i.e., the death penalty is an excessive and unnecessary punishment that violates the 8th amendment.

Justices Douglas, White, and Stewart did not go as far as Brennan and Marshall. The common ground in the opinions of these three justices was the idea that the administration of the death penalty under existing state laws that gave juries unlimited discretion in imposing the death penalty was unconstitutional. Though wanting the Court to end capital punishment entirely, Brennan and Marshall joined Douglas, White, and Stewart in the per curiam opinion holding that the "imposition and carrying out" of the death penalty was, under the procedures used in the *Furman, Jackson*, and *Branch* trials, unconstitutional.

In his opinion, Justice Douglas wrote:

In a nation committed to equal protection of the laws there is no permissible "caste" aspect of law enforcement. Yet we know that the discretion of judges and juries in imposing the death penalty enables the penalty to be selectively applied, feeding prejudices against the accused if he is poor and despised, lacking political clout, or if he is a member of a suspect or unpopular minority, and saving those who by social position may be in a more protected position. . . . The high service rendered by the "cruel and unusual" punishment clause of the 8th amendment is to require legislatures to write penal laws that are even handed, non-selective, and non-arbitrary, and to require judges to see to it that general laws are not applied sparsely, selectively and spottily to unpopular groups. . . . Thus these discretionary statutes are unconstitutional in their operation. They are pregnant with discrimination and discrimination is an ingredient not compatible with the idea of equal protection of the laws that is implicit in the ban on "cruel and unusual" punishments.

Justice White's opinion focused on how rarely executions were carried out: "The death penalty could so seldom be imposed that it would cease to be a credible deterrent or measurably to contribute to any other end of punishment in the criminal justice system. . . . A penalty with such negligible returns to the state would be patently excessive and cruel and unusual punishment."

Justice Stewart wrote:

These death sentences are cruel and unusual in the same way that being struck by lightning is cruel and unusual. For all the people convicted of rapes and murders are among a capriciously selected random handful upon whom the sentence of death has in fact been imposed. . . . I simply conclude that the 8th and 14th amendments cannot tolerate the infliction of a sentence of death under legal systems that permit this unique penalty to be so wantonly and so freakishly imposed.

But Stewart did not rule out that the death penalty would comply with the Eighth Amendment if a fairer system of imposing capital punishment could be established.

Chief Justice Burger wrote a strong dissenting opinion that criticized the per curiam decision as a break with legal precedent. He was critical of the Court for what seemed to be a reversal of opinion from its decision in *McGautha v. California* (1971) the previous year. In *McGautha*, the Court, by a 6–3 vote, upheld the statutes of California and Ohio, which gave juries broad discretion in death penalty sentencing. It appeared that justices Stewart and White may have changed their minds since *McGautha*.

Burger went on to point out that "capital punishment is authorized by statute in 40 states," and that many states would attempt to amend their death penalty statutes to conform to the *Furman* decision. Burger complained, "Since there is no majority of the Court on the ultimate issue presented in these cases, the future of capital punishment in this country has been left in an uncertain limbo."

Justice Blackmun's opinion focused on the authority of the Supreme Court. He felt that any action to abolish the death penalty should be left to the legislative body of government. He wrote:

Were I a legislator, I would vote against the death penalty. . . . Having lived in a state [Minnesota] which does not have the death penalty. . . . [T]he State, purely from a statistical deterrence point of view, was neither worse nor better for its abolition (of the death penalty). I do not sit on these cases, however,

Chief Justice Warren Burger wrote a opinion that strongly criticized the per curiam decision in Furman v. Georgia, *arguing that the Court's decision to overturn Furman's death sentence broke with legal precedent.*

*as a legislator. I trust the Court fully appreci-
ates what it is doing when it decides these
cases the way it does today. Not only are the
capital punishment laws of 39 states and the
District of Columbia struck down, but also
all those provisions of the federal statutory
structure . . . are voided. No longer is capital
punishment possible . . . for treason or assas-
sination of the President.*

Justice Powell wrote a scholarly opinion generally criticizing the per curiam decision. He argued
that none of the majority opinions established a
"constitutionally adequate foundation for the
court's decision" and that the "Court also brushes
aside an unbroken line of precedent reaffirming the
heretofore virtually unquestioned constitutionality
of capital punishment." Like Burger and Blackmun,
Powell worried that the Court was overstepping its
boundaries, stating: "The second consideration dic-
tating judicial self-restraint arises from a proper
recognition of the respective roles of the legislative
and judicial branches. The designation of punishments for crimes is a matter peculiarly within the
sphere of the state and federal legislative bodies."

Justice Rehnquist's opinion also focused on the
role of the judiciary and the need for judicial
restraint. He commented, "The Court's judgments
today strike down a penalty that our Nation's legislators have thought necessary since our country
was founded. . . . Whatever its precise rationale,
today's holding necessarily brings into sharp relief
the fundamental question of the role of judicial
review in a democratic society."

The decisions in the Furman cases generated
substantial and widespread publicity. The *New York
Times* carried a banner front-page headline that

trumpeted: SUPREME COURT, 5–4, BARS DEATH PENAL-
TY AS IT IS IMPOSED UNDER PRESENT STATUTES. The
author of the article observed:

> *The effect of the decision appeared to rule out
> executions under any capital punishment
> laws now in effect in this country. The deci-
> sion will also save from execution 600 con-
> demned men and women now on death rows
> in the United States, although it did not
> overturn their convictions. Most will be held
> in prison for the rest of their lives, but under
> some states' procedures, some of the prisoners
> may eventually gain their freedom.*
>
> *The decision pitted the five holdovers of
> the more liberal Warren Court [referring to
> former Chief Justice Earl Warren] against
> the four appointees of President Nixon, who
> dissented.*[8]

The *Furman* decision was a victory for those
condemned persons on death row whose lives were
spared. It was only a limited victory for the capital
punishment abolitionists, however, because the
death penalty was still alive as a concept. *Furman*
was a bitter defeat for law-enforcement supporters,
but they viewed it as only a temporary defeat. The
death penalty was not dead yet.

As Chief Justice Burger predicted, many of the
individual state legislatures throughout the country took immediate action to amend their statutes
to conform with what the legislators thought the
Supreme Court had held in *Furman v. Georgia*.

Chapter 6

THE IMPACT OF FURMAN

William Henry Furman, whose case clarified whether the death penalty constituted cruel and unusual punishment, has returned to anonymity. He was released from the Georgia State Penitentiary on parole in 1984 and discharged from parole in 1988.[1] He may not be happy with the way his life turned out, but he is at least alive to consider the matter.

Furman v. Georgia, however, did not fade away. It shook the foundations of the criminal justice system. In response to the decision, thirty-five state legislatures had amended statutes by 1976 in an attempt to comply with the Supreme Court's rather murky holding in *Furman.*[2] Some states adopted laws that required a mandatory death sentence for conviction of certain crimes. Other states passed laws that provided detailed criteria to guide judges and juries in imposing the death penalty. In 1976, the Supreme Court agreed to review five capital punishment cases that challenged the new capital punishment laws in several states. Its ruling would possibly determine the fate of the death penalty in the United States.

Three of the 1976 cases—*Gregg v. Georgia*, *Profitt v. Florida*, and *Jurek v. Texas*—involved statutes that gave judges and juries clearer sentencing standards. (This approach to capital sentencing is generally known as guided discretion.) The other two cases—*Woodson v. North Carolina* and *Roberts v. Louisiana*—involved state laws that required mandatory death sentences after conviction of specified crimes.

Gregg v. Georgia was designated as the lead case of the three guided discretion cases. Following the Court's decision in *Furman v. Georgia*, the Georgia state legislature had amended its death penalty statutes. The new law provided that after a person was found guilty of a capital offense, a presentence hearing would be held at which the judge or jury should hear additional evidence in extenuation, mitigation, and aggravation of punishment, including the record of any prior convictions or absence of prior convictions. At least one of ten aggravating circumstances must be proven beyond a reasonable doubt before the defendant could be sentenced to death.

Troy Gregg had been convicted of first-degree murder of two victims, who were killed during the course of a robbery in Gwinnett County, Georgia. Following Georgia's new capital sentencing procedure, the jury found two aggravating circumstances contained in the statute and sentenced Gregg to death. The Georgia Supreme Court affirmed the judgment.

The U.S. Supreme Court granted a petition for a writ of certiorari in order to review the case. The composition of the Supreme Court had changed since *Furman*. Justice Douglas had retired, and President Gerald Ford had appointed Justice John Paul Stevens to the Court. A native of Illinois, Stevens had graduated first in his class from the University of Chicago. He had clerked for Supreme Court Justice Wiley B. Rutledge after graduating from Northwestern Law School and was serving on the U.S. Court of Appeals when appointed to the Supreme Court.

On July 2, 1976, the Supreme Court attempted to settle the unsettled and sometimes volatile death penalty situation. The Supreme Court voted to affirm Gregg's conviction, but the justices could not agree on one opinion. Three justices—Stewart, Powell, and Stevens—supported the opinion written by Justice Stewart. Three others— White, Burger, and Rehnquist—supported a separate opinion authored by Justice White. Justice Blackmun concurred in the final judgment but not in either of these two opinions. Justices Brennan and Marshall dissented, writing in separate opinions that the death penalty was cruel and unusual punishment and, therefore, unconstitutional.

Despite significant disagreements, the seven-member majority agreed that the death penalty did *not*, under all circumstances, constitute cruel and unusual punishment. The majority generally approved of the Georgia statute, which provided for a consideration of aggravating and mitigating factors when determining a death sentence. The Georgia statute in question provided:

(a) The death penalty may be imposed for the offenses of aircraft hijacking or treason, in any case.
(b) In all cases of other offenses for which the death penalty may be authorized, the judge

shall consider, or he shall include in his instructions to the jury for it to consider, any mitigating circumstances or aggravating circumstances otherwise authorized by law and any of the following statutory aggravating circumstances which may be supported by the evidence:

(1) The offense of murder, rape, armed robbery, or kidnapping was committed by a person with a prior record of conviction for a capital felony, or the offense of murder was committed by a person who has a substantial history of serious assaultive criminal convictions.

(2) The offense of murder, rape, armed robbery, or kidnapping was committed while the offender was engaged in the commission of another capital felony, or aggravated battery, or the offense of murder was committed while the offender was engaged in the commission of burglary or arson in the first degree.

(3) The offender by his act of murder, armed robbery, or kidnapping knowingly created a great risk of death to more than one person in a public place by means of a weapon or device which would normally be hazardous to the lives of more than one person.

(4) The offender committed the offense of murder for himself or another, for the purpose of receiving money or any other thing of monetary value.

(5) The murder of a judicial officer, former judicial officer, district attorney or solicitor or former district attorney or solicitor during or because of the exercise of his official duty.

(6) The offender caused or directed anoth-

er to commit murder or committed murder
as an agent or employee of another person.

(7) The offense of murder, rape, armed
robbery, or kidnapping was outrageously or
wantonly vile, horrible or inhuman in that it
involved torture, depravity of mind, or an
aggravated battery to the victim.

(8) The offense of murder was committed
against any peace officer, corrections employee or fireman while engaged in the performance of his official duties.

(9) The offense of murder was committed
by a person in, or who has escaped from, the
lawful custody of a peace officer or place of
lawful confinement.

(10) The murder was committed for the
purpose of avoiding, interfering with, or preventing a lawful arrest or custody in a place
of lawful confinement of himself or another.

(c) The statutory instructions as determined
by the trial judge to be warranted by the evidence shall be given in the charge and in
writing to the jury for its deliberation. The
jury, if its verdict be a recommendation of
death, shall designate in writing, signed by
the foreman of the jury, the aggravating circumstances or circumstances which it found
beyond a reasonable doubt. In non-jury cases
the judge shall make such designation.
Except in cases of treason or aircraft hijacking, unless at least one of the statutory
aggravating circumstances . . . is so found,
the death penalty shall not be imposed.

By upholding the Georgia statute in Gregg, the
Court indicated that it would approve death penalty laws that provided certain conditions: clear stan-

dards to guide juries in their sentencing decisions, a consideration of any mitigating factors, and an automatic review of each death sentence in a state court of appeals.[3]

The Supreme Court sought to clarify its position in Gregg's companion cases. In *Jurek v. Texas*, the Court considered a Texas law similar to the Georgia law in *Gregg* and found it constitutional.[4] Anthony G. Amsterdam, the same attorney who argued the *Furman* case, represented Jurek. The justices voted with the same division as in *Gregg*. In *Profitt v. Florida*, the Supreme Court approved a Florida law that was similar to the Georgia law except that the trial judge was authorized to impose the sentence after considering certain aggravating and mitigating circumstances.[5]

The Court viewed the two cases involving mandatory death sentences much differently. In *Woodson v. North Carolina* and *Roberts v. Louisiana*, the Supreme Court struck down state laws that imposed a mandatory death penalty for anyone convicted of first-degree murder. The 5–4 majority stressed that mandatory sentences in the United States had become very rare. The majority viewed automatic death sentences as inconsistent with "evolving standards of decency" and ruled that such sentences constituted cruel and unusual punishment under the Eighth Amendment. In *Woodson* and *Roberts*, Justices Stewart, Powell, and Stevens were joined by justices Brennan and Marshall, although Brennan and Marshall restated their position that the death penalty was cruel and unusual under all circumstances. Justices White, Burger, Rehnquist, and Blackmun dissented.[6]

The *Gregg, Jurek, Profitt, Woodson,* and *Roberts* decisions attempted to answer many questions left unanswered by the *Furman* decision. The Court's rulings in these five cases have become strong precedents that have remained largely intact. Much to the disappointment of capital punishment abolitionists, these cases firmly established the concept of the constitutionality of the death penalty. The Court generally approved criteria to guide judges and juries in determining whether the death penalty should be applied. These cases permitted future courts to decide whether the death penalty was excessive for certain crimes or when there were unusual circumstances.

Justice Stewart wrote in his *Gregg v. Georgia* opinion:

> *We now hold that the punishment of death does not invariably violate the Constitution. . . . The history of the prohibition of "cruel and unusual" punishment already has been reviewed at length. The phrase first appeared in the English Bill of Rights of 1689 which was drafted by Parliament at the accession of William and Mary. . . . American draftsmen who adopted the English phrasing in drafting the 8th amendment were primarily concerned . . . with proscribing "torture" and other "barbarous" methods of punishment.*

In several decisions following *Gregg*, the Supreme Court found unconstitutional other state laws that required mandatory death sentences upon conviction of specified crimes. In *Coker v. Georgia* (1977) the Supreme Court declared that a sentence of death for the commission of a rape was disproportionate and excessive. At the time, Georgia was the only state to punish rape by death.[7] In *Eberheart v. Georgia*, an opinion handed down at the same time as *Coker*, the Court over-

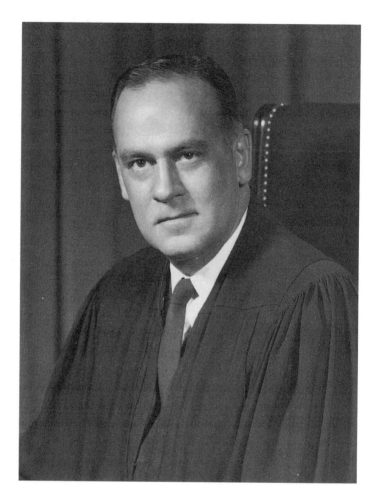

Justice Potter Stewart joined the majority in Gregg v. Georgia *(1976), which ruled that the death penalty did not, under all circumstances, constitute cruel and unusual punishment. After the Supreme Court had ruled in* Furman *that Georgia's capital punishment procedures were unconstitutional, the state revised its laws to give juries more guidance in determining whether to impose the death penalty .The Court upheld these new laws in* Gregg.

turned the imposition of the death penalty for kid-napping when no murder took place.[8] In *Sumner v. Shuman* (1987), the Court found unconstitutional a mandatory-type state law that required an auto-matic death penalty for any murder committed by a life prisoner.[9]

The Supreme Court considered several cases involving the question of whether the death penalty was appropriate for an accomplice, a person who participates in a crime. An accomplice, sometimes called an aider and abettor, can be found guilty of murder under the felony-murder doctrine, regard-less of intent, if he or she participates in the felony that results in death. In *Lockett v. Ohio* (1978), the defendant was involved in the planning and rob-bing of a pawnshop, but she remained in the car while her brother and a friend actually went into the pawnshop. The pawnbroker grabbed for the gun and it went off, killing the pawnbroker. Sandra Lockett was given the death penalty as an aider and abettor. The majority opinion of Chief Justice Burger found the Ohio statute invalid because it limited the range of mitigating factors that could be considered by the jury.[10] In *Enmund v. Florida* (1982), the Court ruled that the death penalty was excessive for a getaway driver when the active par-ticipants committed a robbery that resulted in death to a victim.[11] In *Tison v. Arizona* (1987), how-ever, the Court held that an active participant in a robbery was guilty of murder under the felony-mur-der doctrine and that the death penalty was appro-priate. The two defendants in *Tison* were sons of the triggerman, helped their father escape from prison, and were present when their father deliber-ately killed an innocent family of four. The Supreme Court found that the sons had demonstrated "a reckless indifference to human life."[12] Whether the death penalty is appropriate for an accomplice seems to depend on the extent of his or her participation.

In *Thompson v. Oklahoma* (1988), the Supreme Court held that a person should not be executed if he or she was under the age of sixteen when the crime was committed.[13] One year later, the Court ruled in *Stanford v. Kentucky* (1989) that the death penalty is constitutional for a defendant who was sixteen when he committed the crime.[14]

In *Ford v. Wainwright* (1986), the Court held that it "offends humanity" to execute a person who had become insane after sentence but before execution.[15] Later, in *Penry v. Lynaugh* (1989), the Court ruled that it was not cruel and unusual to execute a mentally retarded defendant.[16]

The Supreme Court has rejected the argument of proportionality: that a particular defendant received the death penalty when defendants in similar cases generally did not receive the death penalty. In *Pulley v. Harris* (1984), Robert A. Harris, a black defendant, was convicted of murdering two young white men and sentenced to death. He petitioned the federal District Court for a writ of habeas corpus alleging that the California statute was unconstitutional because it failed to require the California Supreme Court to compare his sentence to sentences in other death penalty cases to determine whether his sentence was disproportionate. The U.S. Supreme Court rejected this contention and ruled that state laws do not have to require comparative proportionality review.[17]

In *McCleskey v. Kemp* (1984), Warren McCleskey, a black defendant, was convicted of killing a white police officer during a robbery and sentenced to death. McCleskey appealed his sentence. To support their arguments, McCleskey's lawyers offered a scientific study of 2,000 murder cases in

Georgia in the 1970s. The study produced several striking results:

1. defendants convicted of murdering white victims received the death penalty in 11 percent of the cases; defendants convicted of murdering black victims received the death penalty in 1 percent of the cases.
2. the death penalty was given in 22 percent of the cases involving black defendants and white victims, in 8 percent of the cases involving white defendants and white victims, in 3 percent of the cases involving white defendants and black victims, and in 1 percent of the cases involving black defendants and black victims.
3. prosecutors sought the death penalty in 70 percent of the cases involving black defendants and white victims; in 32 percent of the cases involving white defendants and white victims; in 19 percent of the cases involving white defendants and black victims; and in 15 percent of the cases involving black defendants and black victims.[18]

In a 5–4 vote, the Supreme Court rejected the defendant's argument, commenting that "each jury is unique in its composition and the Constitution requires that its decision rest on considerations of innumerable factors that vary according to the characteristics of the individual defendant and the facts of the particular case." In order to demonstrate that his constitutional rights had been violated, McCleskey would have had to "prove that decisionmakers in his case acted with discriminatory purpose."[19]

In *Harris v. Alabama* (1995), the Supreme Court

approved a state statute that authorized the trial judge to sentence a defendant to death but only after consideration of an advisory jury verdict. In this case, the advisory jury recommended life imprisonment but the judge sentenced the defendant to death. The vote on this case was 8–1, with Justice Stevens filing the sole dissent.[20]

Since the *Furman* and *Gregg* decisions, the composition of the Supreme Court has drastically changed through retirements and new appointments, but the Court has pursued a consistent course of supporting the death penalty. The death penalty for serious crimes is not cruel and unusual. State laws that provide a judge or jury with a choice to impose the death penalty based upon a consideration of certain aggravating and mitigating factors are constitutional.

Justice Blackmun retired from the Court in 1994. He had dissented in *Furman*, voicing his opinion that the abolition of the death penalty should be left to the legislature. Before his retirement, Blackmun apparently changed his mind, indicating that he might vote to abolish capital punishment as cruel and unusual. In a dissenting opinion in *Stansbury v. California* (1994), Blackmun wrote, "The death penalty cannot be imposed fairly within the constraints of our Constitution."[21] In *Callins v Collins* (1994), Justice Blackmun strongly dissented in the denial of certiorari to a death penalty case with a long opinion that ended:

> *Perhaps one day this Court will develop procedural rules or verbal formulas that actually provide consistency, fairness, and reliability in a capital sentencing scheme. I am not optimistic that such a day will come. I am more optimistic, though, that this Court eventually*

In 1987, a minister visits with a death-row inmate at a federal penitentiary in Baltimore, Maryland. After the Supreme Court had established the constitutional requirements of death penalty laws with its decision in Gregg *and its companion cases, death-row inmates once again faced the prospect of execution.*

will conclude that the effort to eliminate arbitrariness while preserving fairness in the infliction of death is plainly deemed a failure that it—and the death penalty—must be abandoned altogether. . . . I may not live to see that day, but I have faith that eventually

91

it will arrive. The path the Court has chosen lessens us all.[22]

Justice Stewart's opinion in *Gregg v. Georgia* suggests that the provisions for capital sentencing in the Model Penal Code (MPC) satisfy the Eighth Amendment. Created by legal scholars and other experts, the MPC is a model statute that state legislators can use as a guide when they draft criminal laws for their state. Legislatures typically modify the provisions of MPC to meet their particular local needs or adopt only selected parts of the MPC. Seeking to reduce the likelihood that a capricious, arbitrary, or unfair sentence will be imposed, the MPC's provisions for capital sentencing give guidance to the sentencing authority (judge or jury). The MPC proposes that the following aggravating and mitigating circumstances should be considered during a capital sentencing proceeding:

> *(3) Aggravating Circumstances.*
>   *(a) The murder was committed by a convict under sentence of imprisonment.*
>   *(b) The defendant was previously convicted of another murder or of a felony involving the use or threat of violence to the person.*
>   *(c) At the time the murder was committed the defendant also committed another murder.*
>   *(d) The defendant knowingly created a great risk of death to many persons.*
>   *(e) The murder was committed while the defendant was engaged or was an accomplice in the commission of, or an attempt to commit, or flight from committing or attempting to commit robbery, rape or deviant sexual intercourse by force or threat of force, arson, burglary or kidnapping.*

(f) The murder was committed for the purpose of avoiding or preventing a lawful arrest or effecting an escape from lawful custody.

(g) The murder was committed for pecuniary gain.

(h) The murder was especially heinous, atrocious or cruel, manifesting exceptional depravity.

(4) Mitigating Circumstances.

(a) The defendant has no significant history of prior criminal activity.

(b) The murder was committed while the defendant was under the influence of extreme mental or emotional disturbance.

(c) The victim was a participant in the defendant's homicidal conduct or consented to the homicidal act.

(d) The murder was committed under circumstances which the defendant believed to provide a moral justification or extenuation for his conduct.

(e) The defendant was an accomplice in a murder committed by another person and his participation in the homicidal act was relatively minor.

(f) The defendant acted under duress or under the domination of another person.

(g) At the time of the murder, the capacity of the defendant to appreciate the criminality (wrongfulness) of his conduct or to conform his conduct to the requirements of law was impaired as a result of mental disease or defect or intoxication.

(h) The youth of the defendant at the time of the crime.

Death penalty states have adopted some or all of these guidelines in their capital sentencing laws. The Supreme Court's decision in *Gregg v. Georgia* appears to indicate that a death sentence imposed under procedures that give judges or juries adequate guided discretion does not constitute cruel and unusual punishment.

Chapter 7
THE DEATH PENALTY TODAY

At the time of the *Furman* decision in 1972, nine states—Alaska, Hawaii, Iowa, Maine, Michigan, Minnesota, Oregon, West Virginia, and Wisconsin—had completely abolished the death penalty. Following the *Furman* decision, Oregon once again reinstated the death penalty. Five states—New Mexico, New York, North Dakota, Rhode Island, and Vermont—were considered de facto abolition states in 1972 because the death penalty was highly restricted. New York, for example, had partially abolished the death penalty in 1965, except for the killing of a peace officer and the murder of a guard by a prisoner serving a life sentence. In 1995, the New York legislature enacted a death penalty for first-degree murder.

Massachusetts had its death penalty invalidated by *Furman*. The state legislature redrafted a death penalty statute in 1979, but that statute was then found unconstitutional by the Massachusetts Supreme Court. Because no further legislative action has occurred following the court's decision, Massachusetts currently has no death penalty.

Here is a breakdown of states by category from the time of the *Furman* decision until now. All of the states not mentioned below had the death penalty at the time of *Furman*, then passed new death penalty laws with provisions intended to conform with the *Furman* ruling.

Abolition states (1972)	Abolition states (1996)	Death Penalty States (1996)
Alaska	Alaska	
Hawaii	Hawaii	
Iowa		Iowa
Maine	Maine	
Michigan	Michigan	
Minnesota	Minnesota	
Oregon		Oregon
West Virginia	West Virginia	
Wisconsin	Wisconsin	
	Massachusetts	
	District of Columbia	

Restrictive Death (1972)	Restrictive Death (1996)	Death Penalty (1996)
New Mexico		New Mexico
New York		New York
North Dakota	North Dakota	
Rhode Island	Rhode Island	
Vermont	Vermont	

In 1996, thirty-eight states had the death penalty. Twelve states and the District of Columbia either did not have the death penalty or had a highly restricted death penalty.

The death penalty has emerged as an important

issue in some political campaigns. In the U.S. senatorial election in California in 1982, Pete Wilson supported the death penalty against two-term former governor Jerry Brown. Wilson won. In 1986, Chief Justice Rose Bird of the California Supreme Court and two associate justices who supported her were recalled by popular vote. Bird was on record as opposing the death penalty. In reviewing criminal convictions in which defendants received the death penalty, she voted to reverse sixty-one or more death sentences that came before the California Supreme Court. Many Californians thought that Chief Justice Bird was deliberately finding judicial errors to support her personal opinion in opposition to the death penalty.

In the 1988 presidential election, the Democratic candidate, Michael Dukakis, opposed the death penalty while the Republican candidate, Vice President George Bush, supported it. Bush campaigned heavily on the law-enforcement issue, criticizing Dukakis for leniency in releasing prisoners while governor of Massachusetts. Bush won the election.

Mario Cuomo was elected governor of New York in 1982 and vowed that no one would be executed while he was governor. On several occasions, the state legislature enacted death penalty laws only to have Cuomo veto them. Cuomo was defeated in 1994 by George Pataki, who stressed his support of the death penalty during the gubernatorial campaign.

In the 1992 presidential election, Bill Clinton made certain that the voters knew he supported the death penalty. After taking office, Clinton continued to support the death penalty, as did Bob Dole and the other candidates in the 1996 Republican presidential primary.

EXECUTIONS AND THEIR COSTS

Gary Gilmore was the first person executed after *Gregg* had established the constitutional requirements of death penalty laws. Gilmore, who had been convicted of robbing and murdering a motel night clerk while on parole, was executed by a Utah firing squad on the cold winter morning of January 17, 1977. He had decided not to fight his execution through legal appeals, reasoning, "I would definitely prefer a quick death to a slow life in the joint." This made Gilmore a near folk hero to some people. It was the first execution carried out in the United States since June 2, 1967.

There were no executions the following year, but the rate of executions began to gain momentum. In 1979, John Spenkelink was scheduled for execution in Florida. Spenkelink had been serving a five-year sentence for armed robbery in California when he escaped from a conservation camp. While driving through Nebraska, he picked up an Ohio parole violator. After the two men arrived in Florida, Spenkelink killed his companion, claiming self-defense. Spenkelink was found guilty and sentenced to death. He fought his execution with every conceivable legal tactic. His attorneys filed twenty-two unsuccessful appeals. His defenders claimed Spenkelink had been rehabilitated after six years in prison and requested clemency. The clemency appeal was turned down, and Governor Bob Graham signed the death warrant while protesters outside the governor's mansion shouted "Bloody Bob!"

Time magazine recounted the execution ritual: "[Spenkelink] was strapped tightly into the stout oak chair, a black gag across his mouth. Suddenly a black hood dropped over his face, and six attendants stepped back. The executioner, his identity a

In December 1976, Utah officials escort Gary Gilmore into court for a hearing to determine a date for his execution. On January 17, 1977, Gilmore, who chose not to appeal his death sentence, became the first person executed in the United States since 1967.

secret and his face also shrouded in black, flipped a red switch, sending 2,250 volts of electricity through the man's body, then two more surges." The *Time* article went on to describe the attendant publicity "as 130 other condemned men on Florida's death row shouted and pounded on cell bars. Some 70 demonstrators gathered on a field near the prison chanting 'Death row must go' and singing 'We shall overcome.' "[1]

Executions in the United States Since 1977

Year	Number of executions
1977	1
1978	0
1979	2
1980	0
1981	1
1982	2
1983	3
1984	21
1985	18
1986	18
1987	25
1988	11
1989	16
1990	23
1991	14
1992	31
1993	34
1994	31
1995	56

Virtually all executions in the United States have been protested by groups and individuals

John Spenkelink fought to have his death sentence overturned by using every possible legal tactic. He was executed in Florida in 1979.

opposed to the death penalty, but on at least one occasion those protesting against the execution were outnumbered by those in favor of the execution. As dawn broke on January 24, 1989, about three hundred people gathered outside Raiford

State Prison, in Starke, Florida, to await the execution of Theodore Bundy. Bundy had been convicted of murdering two young female college students and a third young girl and was a suspect in nearly fifty other murders of young women throughout the United States. Cheers went up from the waiting crowd when it was announced that Bundy had been executed.

Public opinion on capital punishment has fluctuated through the years. In Gallup Poll surveys conducted annually from 1936 to 1995, the percentage of persons in favor of the death penalty ranged from a low of 42 percent in 1966 to a high of 80 percent in 1994. The percentage of persons opposed to the death penalty ranged from a high of 47 percent in 1966 to a low of 13 percent in 1995.[2]

Since *Furman*, Congress has enacted laws that authorize the death penalty in the killing of any federal, state, or local law enforcement officer engaged in the performance of the officer's duty. Other new federal laws authorize the death penalty in cases of espionage by a member of the armed forces, witness tampering where death occurs, death resulting from aircraft hijacking, and murder intentionally committed by a person engaging in a drug-related felony offense. In 1994, Congress passed the Violent Crime Control and Law Enforcement Act, a major crime bill that expands the federal death penalty to cover about sixty offenses.[3]

According to the U.S. Bureau of Prisons, no one has been executed for a federal offense since 1963. In 1996, there were seven federal prisoners on death row for civilian offenses and eight military prisoners on death row. The federal government has no execution facility but is authorized to use state prisons. The Bureau of Prisons plans to establish a death row and execution chamber at its Terre Haute, Indiana, federal prison. It will use the lethal injection method of execution.

From 1977 until January 1, 1995, 4,557 persons received the death penalty in state courts; 51 percent were white, 40 percent were black, 7 percent

A List of Executions by State (1976–1995)	
Texas	106
Florida	35
Virginia	32
Louisiana	23
Georgia	20
Missouri	19
Alabama	13
Arkansas	11
Delaware	8
North Carolina	8
Illinois	7
Oklahoma	7
Nevada	6
South Carolina	5
Utah	5
Mississippi	4
Arizona	4
Indiana	3
California	3
Washington	2
Pennsylvania	2
Idaho	1
Maryland	1
Nebraska	1
Wyoming	1
Montana	1

were Hispanic, and 2 percent were of some other background or race. Out of this number, 257 were executed, and 1,790 had their sentences or convictions overturned or died while waiting on death row. The number of persons on death row as of October 1995 was 3,046.

The methods of administering the death penalty have changed with the advance of technology. At least twenty-seven states now execute by lethal injection, and there is a growing trend in that direction. Utah now permits execution by lethal injection or by firing squad, with the defendant given the macabre choice. In October 1994, U.S. district judge Marilyn Hall Patel ordered the State of California to conduct all future executions by lethal injections. Judge Patel heard from a battery of scientific experts and examined a half century of official executions during an eight-day trial in San Francisco. She found that prisoners in the gas chamber are likely to suffer excruciating pain for between fifteen seconds and several minutes. Judge Patel's ruling barring execution in the state gas chamber was upheld by a federal appeals court of three judges, voting 3–0.

California was ready for this decision. In 1993, the California legislature had passed a bill to authorize the use of lethal injection. At 2:01 A.M. on February 23, 1996, William Bonin, the so-called Freeway Killer, was executed by lethal injection for the murders of fourteen young men and boys. Bonin earned his gruesome nickname by dumping the naked body of each victim alongside freeways in Los Angeles and Orange counties. Bonin became the first person in California to be executed by lethal injection. At 10:45 P.M. the night before the execution, the U.S. Supreme Court rejected a request for a stay of execution, and Governor Pete Wilson rejected a request for clemency. Ironically, the lethal injection execution was carried out in the gas chamber facility at San Quentin Prison.

Most death penalty convictions are appealed, and this is a lengthy and costly process with appointed attorneys for defendants. Some cases on appeal have gone on for more than ten years. Opponents of the death penalty argue that lengthening the process prolongs the agony of the prisoner, prolonging the cruelty. Supporters of the death penalty blame the prisoners themselves for extending the appeal process. In other words, the prisoners cause their own cruelty by appealing. The U.S. Bureau of Prisons calculated that the average time spent between sentence and execution for prisoners executed between 1977 and 1994 was eight years. The thirty-one prisoners executed in 1994 were under sentence of death an average of more than ten years.

A continuing controversy concerns the length of time between conviction and execution. The environment on death row tends to generate legal actions by prisoners. The prisoner has plenty of time and usually has access to a law library, and the death sentence provides strong motivation to take action. Some prisoners, such as California prisoner Caryl Chessman, become legal experts while working on their own cases and advising other prisoners. The normal pattern for appeals taken by a convicted person who has been sentenced to death is:

1. appeal to the state supreme court
2. if the state court affirms the death sentence, file a petition for a writ of habeas corpus in the appropriate federal district court
3. if the federal district court affirms the death sentence, file an appeal with the appropriate federal court of appeals
4. if the federal court of appeals confirms the

death sentence, petition the U.S. Supreme
Court for a writ of certiorari
5. if the petition for a writ of certiorari is
denied, file a petition for a writ of habeas
corpus in the appropriate federal district
court alleging a new and different violation
of constitutional rights

The appeal process involves substantial costs for
appointed attorneys for the defendant, for government attorneys to oppose the defendants' legal
actions, and for judicial administration. Justice
Powell alluded to this issue in his concurring opinion in *Schneckloth v. Bustamonte* (1973), a case in
which the petition for writ of habeas corpus alleged
that evidence should have been excluded because it
was obtained by unreasonable search and seizure.
Powell felt the scope of inquiry in a petition for writ
of habeas corpus had expanded far beyond the original intent, commenting, "Those [legal system]
resources are limited but demand on them con-
stantly increases. . . . After all, the resources of our
[legal] system are finite: their over-extension jeop-
ardizes the care and quality essential to fair adjudi-
cation. . . . Finally, the present scope of habeas
corpus tends to undermine the values inherent in
our federal system of government."[4]

Warren McCleskey provides an excellent example of the length, and thereby cost, of the death
penalty appeals process. He was convicted of murder and sentenced to death in 1978. He filed a petition for a writ of habeas corpus in a federal district
court, claiming that the state sentencing process
was administered in a racially discriminatory manner. The U.S. Supreme Court denied his appeal in
McCleskey v. Kemp (1984).[5]

The same Warren McCleskey filed a new petition for a writ of habeas corpus, claiming a new violation of his constitutional rights that his lawyers had not raised in his first appeal. The defendants in both cases were the superintendents of the Georgia Diagnostic & Classification Center (Kemp had been succeeded by Zant). In *McCleskey v. Zant* (1991), the Supreme Court rejected McCleskey's second petition on grounds that he should have litigated this claim in his first appeal as required by federal law. The Court further found that McCleskey's latest claim of constitutional rights violation, "would not affect the reliability of the guilty determination." In his opinion, Justice Kennedy, echoing the thoughts of Justice Powell, wrote, "Habeas corpus review extracts further costs. Federal collateral litigation places a heavy burden on scarce federal judicial resources and threatens the capacity of the system to resolve primary disputes."[6]

In *Coleman v. Thompson* (1991), the Supreme Court denied the defendant's petition for a writ of habeas corpus on procedural grounds. Coleman appealed to the Virginia Supreme Court, and that court rejected his claims. He then filed a petition for writ of habeas corpus in a Virginia circuit court alleging violations under the federal Constitution. The state circuit court considered and denied Coleman's petition after a hearing. Coleman's lawyers failed by three days to appeal within the thirty days required, and Coleman then filed a petition for habeas corpus in a federal district court alleging federal constitutional claims that had already been raised and ruled upon in the state habeas corpus proceedings. The district court ruled on all the claims and denied the petition. A federal court of appeal affirmed the district court's ruling. The U.S. Supreme Court denied Coleman's claim on procedural grounds that the Virginia courts had ruled on the defendant's federal constitutional claims and that Coleman had not appealed the state court's decision within the thirty-day requirement.

Justice Blackmun dissented, along with Justices Marshall and Stevens. Blackmun wrote:

> *The Court today continues its crusade to erect petty procedural barriers in the path of any state prisoner seeking review of his federal constitutional claims. Because I believe that the Court is creating a Byzantine morass of arbitrary, unnecessary and unjustifiable impediments to the vindication of federal rights, I dissent. . . . The Court's habeas [corpus] jurisprudence now routinely, and without evident reflection, subordinates fundamental constitutional rights to mere utilitarian interests. . . . Such unreflective cost-benefit analysis is inconsistent with the very idea of rights.*[7]

In 1992, the Supreme Court denied Coleman's application for a stay of execution in a per curiam opinion, stating, "this is now the twelfth round of judicial review in a murder case which began eleven years ago. Yet despite having had eleven years to produce exculpatory evidence, Coleman has produced what . . . does not even amount to a colorable claim of innocence."[8]

In April 1996, Congress passed and President Clinton signed the Comprehensive Terrorism Prevention Act of 1995, which included some procedural changes for the processing of writs of habeas corpus. These new provisions have a substantial effect on the rights of appeal for persons receiving the death penalty in state courts: Applications for writs of habeas corpus must be filed in a federal district court within one year of a state court's final decision. The federal district judge must act on the writ within six months. If the defendant appeals the decision of the district judge, the federal court of appeals must decide the case within six months. The defendant is entitled to file only one application for a writ of habeas corpus unless there is newly discovered evidence that is clear and convincing proof that the defendant is not guilty. Federal judges may not reverse a state conviction or death sentence unless it resulted from an "unreasonable application of clearly established federal law."

On May 3, 1996, the U.S. Supreme Court, by a 5–4 vote, agreed to hear a constitutional challenge to the new law. Chief Justice Rehnquist, along with Justices Sandra Day O'Connor, Antonin Scalia, Anthony M. Kennedy, and Clarence Thomas, voted for the unusually quick review. Justices John P. Stevens, David H. Souter, Ruth Bader Ginsberg, and Stephen G. Breyer voted against the unusual action with an opinion that a constitutional review of the new law should be "undertaken with the utmost deliberation, rather than unseemly haste."

THE FUTURE OF CAPITAL PUNISHMENT

What is the future of the death penalty? Judging from the long line of Supreme Court cases following *Furman v. Georgia* and *Gregg v. Georgia*, it seems clear that the death penalty will remain in effect for the foreseeable future. The controversy over the issue, however, persists. Abolitionists demonstrate outside prisons when executions take place. The NAACP and other organizations provide legal

In Dead Man Walking *(1993), Sister Helen Prejean wrote about her experiences counseling a Louisiana death-row inmate. Her book, and the 1995 film based on it, focused attention on the death penalty issue.*

defense for indigent defendants charged with death penalty offenses. Statistical arguments continue to show that the death penalty is not a deterrent and that members of minority groups are more likely to receive the death penalty. Abolitionist leaders continue to argue that the death penalty is cruel and unusual and, therefore, unconstitutional under the Eighth Amendment.

The abolition movement was reenergized by Helen Prejean, a Roman Catholic nun in the Sisters of St. Joseph of Medaille order, who wrote the thoughtful book, *Dead Man Walking: An Eyewitness Account of the Death Penalty in the United States* (1993). Sister Prejean had befriended Patrick Sonnier, a convict on death row in Louisiana. *Dead Man Walking* was made into a popular movie in 1995. Susan Sarandon, who portrayed Prejean in the film, won an Academy Award as best actress; Tim Robbins was nominated as best director; and Sean Penn, who portrayed Sonnier, was nominated as best actor.

The supporters of the death penalty, however, maintain the upper hand. Politicians continue to run on platforms supporting the death penalty, and they win elections. Law enforcement officials counter the arguments of the abolitionists, urging that the death penalty be retained for appropriate cases. Public opinion polls tend to show that the majority of Americans favor the death penalty.

No one can accurately predict the future of the death penalty. For certain, the lines between the two camps are firmly drawn and chances for any compromise seem unthinkable. By the end of 1996, supporters of the death penalty seemed to be "winning," but abolitionists have come back again and again. The battle is far from over.

The Death Penalty Debate

The debate over the death penalty is centered around issues of deterrence, protection, retribution, barbarity, irreversibility, fairness, and cost. The typical arguments in support of the death penalty are:

1. *The death penalty is a deterrent to crime.* People will not commit serious crimes if they fear that they will be executed.
2. *The death penalty provides the retribution that society expects.* If there is no death penalty, the families of victims might take the law into their own hands and kill the accused.
3. *Society should be protected against repeated offenses by the same offender in the event the prisoner escapes or is released.*
4. *The death penalty is traditional, and society relies on its protection.* Capital punishment reinforces the idea that society will not tolerate certain types of behavior.
5. *Taxpayers should not be expected to support a criminal in prison for the rest of his or her life.* Even if the costs of the appeals process in death penalty cases are exorbitant, the benefits of capital punishment justify the expense.
6. *The death penalty is supported by biblical text:* "An eye for an eye and a tooth for a tooth." The severity of the punishment should match the seriousness of the crime.

On April 20, 1992, standing outside California's San Quentin State Prison several hours before the execution of Robert Alton Harris three men demonstrate their support for the death penalty.

Arguments against the death penalty include:

1. *The death penalty is barbaric and a relic of the past.* Any type of execution is a form of torture, and the use of capital punishment by the government legitimizes violence.
2. *The death penalty is cruel and unusual and in conflict with the Eighth Amendment of the Constitution.* It is cruel because it causes death. It is unusual because it is rarely imposed
3. *There is a risk of executing an innocent person.* Once an execution has occurred, it cannot be reversed.
4. *The death penalty is not a deterrent.* There is no clear evidence that the death penalty lowers the rate of violent crime. States and nations without the death penalty experience no greater crime rate than those with the death penalty, and studies of the crime rates before and after a state has introduced the death penalty have been inconclusive.
5. *The death penalty is unfair because it is imposed disproportionately on people who are poor, uneducated, or members of a minority group.* African-Americans, for example, make up a considerably larger percentage of the death row population than they do in the general population. The rich are unlikely to be executed because they can employ superior attorneys who can win cases and wield influence for clemency in sentencing.

Outside a state government building in San Francisco, death penalty opponents protest the execution of Robert Alton Harris, which had occurred about six hours earlier.

6. *The implementation of the death penalty is not uniform from case to case and from state to state.* Certain states tend to impose the death penalty more than other states. Some states have no death penalty; others have restricted its application to a small number of crimes.

7. *The death penalty costs too much to maintain.* The costs of death penalty cases have soared in recent decades because of the expense of long, complicated trials and the lengthy appeals process. It now costs more to execute a person that to incarcerate him or her for life.

8. *The death penalty is contrary to the biblical text of the New Testament,* which advocates mercy and forgiving.

SOURCE NOTES

CHAPTER 1
1. Powell v. Alabama, 287 US 45 (1932); *Gideon v. Wainwright*, 372 US 335 (1963).
2. Trial transcript, *Furman v. Georgia*, 408 US 238 (1972).

CHAPTER 2
1. Opinion of Georgia Supreme Court, *Furman v. The State*, 167 S.E. 2d 628 (1969).
2. *Mapp v. Ohio*, 367 US 643 (1961).
3. *Miranda v. Arizona*, 384 US 436 (1966).
4. *Witherspoon v. Illinois*, 391 US 510 (1968).

CHAPTER 3
1. Stephen A. Flanders, *Capital Punishment* (New York: Facts On File, 1991), p. 8.
2. The debate is reprinted in Clarence Darrow, *Clarence Darrow on the Death Penalty* (Chicago: Chicago Historical Bookworks, 1991), pp. 31–32.
3. Flanders, pp. 42–43.
4. Ibid., p. 10.

CHAPTER 4

1. *Powell v. Alabama*, 287 US 45 (1932).
2. *Wilkerson v. Utah*, 99 US 130 (1879).
3. *In re Kemmler*, 136 US 436 (1890).
4. *O'Neil v. Vermont*, 144 US 323 (1892).
5. *Weems v. United States*, 217 US 349 (1910).
6. *Louisiana ex rel. Francis v. Resweber*, 329 US 459 (1947).
7. *Trop v. Dulles*, 356 US 86 (1958).
8. *Robinson v. California*, 370 US 660 (1962).
9. *Powell v. Texas*, 392 US 514 (1968).
10. *Rudolph v. Alabama*, 375 US 889 (1963).
11. *McGautha v. California*, 402 US 183 (1971).
12. *Crampton v. Ohio*, 402 US 183 (1971).

CHAPTER 5

1. Appeal record, *Furman v. Georgia*, 408 US 238 (1972).
2. Ibid.
3. Ibid.
4. Ibid.
5. *Time*, January 24, 1972.
6. Opinion of California Supreme Court, *People v. Anderson*, 6 Cal. 3d 628 (1972).
7. *Furman v. Georgia*, 408 US 238 (1972).
8. *New York Times*, June 30, 1972.

CHAPTER 6

1. Department of Corrections, State of Georgia.
2. Flanders, p. 64.
3. *Gregg v. Georgia*, 428 US 153 (1976).
4. *Jurek v. Texas*, 428 US 262 (1972).
5. *Profitt v. Florida*, 428 US 242 (1976).
6. *Woodson v. North Carolina*, 428 US 280 (1976); *Roberts v. Louisiana*, 428 US 325 (1976).
7. *Coker v. Georgia*, 433 US 584 (1977).
8. *Eberheart v. Georgia*, 433 US 917 (1977).

9. *Sumner v. Shuman*, 483 US 66 (1987).

10. *Lockett v. Ohio*, 438 US 586 (1978).

11. *Enmund v. Florida*, 458 US 782 (1982).

12. *Tison v. Arizona*, 481 US 137 (1987).

13. *Thompson v. Oklahoma*, 487 US 815 (1988).

14. *Stanford v. Kentucky*, 492 US 361 (1989).

15. *Ford v. Wainwright*, 477 US 399 (1986).

16. *Penry v. Lynaugh*, 492 US 302 (1989).

17. *Pulley v. Harris*, 428 US 262 (1984).

18. Nancy R. Jacobs et al., eds., *Capital Punishment: Cruel and Unusual?* (Wylie, TX: Information Plus, 1994), pp. 39–40.

19. *McCleskey v. Kemp*, 481 US 279 (1984).

20. *Harris v. Alabama*, 130 L.Ed. 2d 1004 (1995).

21. *Stansbury v. California*, 128 L.Ed. 2d 293 (1994).

22. *Callins v. Collins*, 127 L.Ed. 2d 435 (1994).

CHAPTER 7

1. *Time*, June 4, 1979.

2. Nancy Jacobs et al., eds., *Capital Punishment: Cruel and Unusual?* (Wylie, TX: Information Plus, 1996), p. 83.

3. Congressional Research Service Report for Congress on Crime Control Act of 1994: Capital Punishment Provisions Summarized.

4. *Schneckloth v. Bustamonte*, 412 US 218 (1973).

5. *McCleskey v. Kemp*, 481 US 279 (1984).

6. *McCleskey v. Zant*, 499 US 467 (1991).

7. *Coleman v. Thompson*, 501 US 722 (1991).

8. *Coleman v. Thompson*, 199 L.Ed. 2d 1 (1992).

FOR FURTHER READING

Darrow, Clarence. *Clarence Darrow on the Death Penalty*. Chicago: Chicago Historical Bookworks, 1991.

Flanders, Stephen A. *Capital Punishment*. New York: Facts On File, 1991.

Herda, D. J. *Furman v. Georgia: The Death Penalty Case*. Springfield, N.J.: Enslow, 1994.

Jacobs, Nancy R., et al., eds. *Capital Punishment: Cruel and Unusual?* Wylie, TX: Information Plus, 1996.

Landau, Elaine. *Teens and the Death Penalty*. Springfield, N.J.: Enslow, 1992.

Prejean, Helen. *Dead Man Walking: An Eyewitness Account of the Death Penalty in the United States*. New York: Random House, 1993.

Siegel, Mark, et al., eds. *Capital Punishment: An Effective Punishment?* Wylie, TX: Information Plus, 1991.

Steins, Richard. *The Death Penalty—Is It Justice?* New York: Twenty-First Century Books, 1993.

Tierney, Kevin. *Darrow: A Biography*. New York: Crowell, 1979.

Tushnet, Mark. *The Death Penalty*. New York: Facts On File, 1993.

Wekesser, Carol, ed. *The Death Penalty: Opposing Viewpoints*. San Diego: Greenhaven Press, 1991.

INDEX

Index

ABOUT THE AUTHORS

Judge Burt Henson is retired from the Ventura County Municipal Court. A graduate of Stanford Law School, he practiced law and served in the California legislature before his judicial appointment.

Ross R. Olney is the author of more than 180 nonfiction and fiction books for young readers. He also writes articles for magazines and has a regular newspaper column.

Both authors live in Ventura, California.